HOW TO STUDY

FIFTH EDITION

BY **RON FRY**

CAREER
PRESS
Franklin Lakes, NJ

HOW TO STUDY, 5ᵀᴴ EDITION
Cover design by Design Solutions
Printed in the U.S.A. by Book-mart Press

To order this title, please call toll-free 1-800-CAREER-1 (NJ and Canada: 201-848-0310) to order using VISA or MasterCard, or for further information on books from Career Press.

CAREER
PRESS

The Career Press, Inc., 3 Tice Road, PO Box 687,
Franklin Lakes, NJ 07417
www.careerpress.com

Library of Congress Cataloging-in-Publication Data

Fry, Ronald W.
    How to study / by Ron Fry. — 5th ed.
        p. cm.
    Includes index.
    ISBN 1-56414-456-9 (paper)
    1. Study skills. I. Title.

LB1049 .F74 2000
371.3'028'1 — dc21   00-031194

Contents

How to Use This Book

> What one knows is, in youth, of little moment; they know enough who know how to learn.
>
> —Henry Adams

LEARNING HOW TO study is learning how to *learn*. And that is, to me, the greatest gift you can ever give yourself.

Having stated that so boldly, I suspect I still have to convince some of you that spending any time trying to master this stuff—studying, learning, reading, note-taking, writing, whatever you call it—is worth your while.

There are, of course, some terrific reasons why you *should* learn how to study, why you *must* learn how to study. But before I start convincing you that developing proper study skills really *is* important—and why—let's figure out exactly what we mean by "study skills" so we're all on the same wavelength.

Yes, *How to Study* includes hints, advice, and techniques for taking notes in class, while you're reading your textbooks, in the library, or even online; how to prepare for tests; and how to organize your study schedule to get the best results in the shortest amount of time. But that's the *last* half of the book. There are essential skills you may think don't even have anything to do with studying, and important steps you need to take right from the start.

Here's where to start

 Learn as though you would never be able to master it; hold it as if you would be in fear of losing it.

— Confucius

Developing great study habits is like a race between you and all your friends around a track. Before you can declare a winner, you have to agree on where the finish line is. In other words, how do you measure your ability to use these skills? What's good? What's poor?

But you can't even start the race until you know where the *starting* line is — especially if it's drawn at a different spot for each of you!

Chapter 1 starts by explaining each study skill and clarifying how each can and should function in your life. Then you have the chance to find your own starting line.

In Chapter 2, you'll learn the importance of where, how, and when you study and start building the study environment that's perfect for *you*. Why is this important? If you've spent three hours reading *Ulysses* with Rage Against the Machine shaking the walls, it's not surprising you're still on page three. Reading about and understanding Bloom's day might have little to do with increasing reading com-prehension, rescheduling your time, or changing books...and a lot more to do with just turning down the volume.

There is no magic elixir in the study habit regimen. If math and science are not your strong suits, memorizing *How to Study* will not transform you into a Nobel Prize-winning physicist. Nobody is great at *every*thing, but everybody is great at *some*thing. So you'll also get a chance to rate the subjects you like and dislike, plus those classes you do best and worst in.

Chapter 2 also introduces some of the "intangibles" in the study equation: your home environment, attitude, motivation, and so forth. If you are dedicated to studying and motivated to achieve certain goals, all the other factors that affect your study habits will fall more naturally into place. A belief in the study ethic is one of the keys to success.

Finally, some generalities about the study process—learning to "read" teachers, developing mentors, dealing with perfectionism, the importance of flexibility—will help you get off to the right start.

Reading and comprehension

Chapter 3 introduces the skills basic to any study process: reading and comprehension. No matter how well you learn to take notes, how familiar you become with your library, how deftly you surf the Web, how doggedly you study for tests, if you are reading poorly (or not enough) and not understanding what you read, life will be difficult.

Becoming a good reader is a skill, one usually acquired early in life. If it's a skill you haven't acquired yet, now is the time! Chapter 3 also points out how your ability to recall ideas, facts, and figures can be significantly increased (quantitatively and qualitatively) with the right practice.

Making up for lost time

To see a significant change in your life, many of you will not need to study *harder,* just *smarter.* This means making better use of your study time — spending the same two, three, or four hours, but accomplishing twice, thrice, or four times what you do now. Chapter 4 introduces the simplest and easiest-to-use organizational and time-management tools you'll ever find — powerful ways to make sure you are always on track, including guidelines to develop both short-term and long-term calendars.

Go to the head of the class

In Chapter 5, I talk about the one experience we all have in common, no matter how old we are: the classroom. I'll help you take better notes, encourage your active participation in class discussions — including pointers on how to overcome the tendency to hide behind the plant in the back of the room — and help you get a lot more out of lectures.

Learning your library

Chapter 6 introduces you to the single most important resource in your study career: your library. You'll learn about the books, periodicals, newspapers, magazines, computer software, videos, audiotapes, and other reference materials available to you, and suggestions for how to find and use them, including an explanation of the Dewey Decimal Classification and Library of Congress systems. I'll also cover, very briefly, the use of online resources and the importance of becoming computer and Internet literate.

So you're not the next Hemingway

I'm convinced that too many of you place the emphasis in "writing papers" on the word "writing." In Chapter 7, I'll introduce you to a remarkably easy way to gather research, take notes, and organize your information. By breaking down any paper, no matter how complex, into easy-to-follow steps, I think you'll find you create papers infinitely better than before—even if you're still no threat to Hemingway (or anybody else) when it comes to writing.

How to "ace" any test

Chapter 8 covers the do's and don'ts of test preparation, including the differences between studying for weekly quizzes, midterms, and final examinations; why last-minute cramming doesn't work (but how to do it if you have no other choice—shame!); studying for and taking different types of tests (multiple choice, true-false, essay, open book, and so on); and how to increase your guessing scores, even which questions to answer first and which to leave for last.

How smart do _you_ study?

How to Study is the most comprehensive study guide ever written—a fundamental, step-by-step approach that _you_ can follow to develop and sharpen your study skills.

If you're struggling through college or graduate school, here's your life preserver.

If you're a high school student planning to attend college, _now_'s your chance to hone your study skills.

If you're heading for trade school, planning to dance, write, paint, not considering college, even if you're ready to drop out of high school at the earliest possible instant, you need *How to Study*.

If you're an adult returning to the classroom after a lengthy absence, there's no substitute for the tips and techniques you will learn in this helpful collection.

So what if you're a really poor student? How smart you are is not the point. *What counts is how smart you study.*

With the possible exception of the two percent of you who qualify as "gifted," the effective study habits *How to Study* teaches will help students of any age.

If your grades are average to good, you will see a definite improvement. If you are on the borderline of the pass/fail range, you will benefit considerably. If good study habits are in place but rusty as a result of years away from the classroom, *How to Study* will be the perfect refresher for you.

And if you *are* one of those "two percent gifted," I *still* think you'll find many helpful techniques in these pages.

Who is this book really for?

While I originally wrote *How to Study* for high school students, I've discovered over the years that I could probably count on both hands the number of such students who actually bought a copy of the book.

The surprise was that so many of the people buying *How to Study* (and writing me reams of letters along the way) were adults. Yes, a number of them were returning to school and saw *How to Study* as a great refresher. And some were long out of school but had figured out that if they could learn *now* the study skills their teachers never taught them (or they never took the time to learn), they'd do better in their careers.

All too many were parents who had the same lament: "How do I get Johnny to read (study, do better on tests, remember more, get better grades)?"

So I want to briefly take the time to address every one of the audiences for this book and discuss some of the factors particular to each of you.

If you're a high school student

You should be particularly comfortable with the format of the book—its relatively short sentences and paragraphs, occasionally humorous (hopefully) headings and subheadings, and the language used. I wrote it with you in mind!

But you should also be *un*comfortable with the fact that you're already in the middle of your school years—the period that will drastically affect, one way or the other, all the *rest* of your school years—*and you still don't know how to study!* Don't lose another minute. Make learning how to study and mastering *all* of the study skills in this book your *absolute priority.*

If you're a junior high school student

Congratulations! You're learning how to study at *precisely* the right time. Sixth, 7th, and 8th grades—before that sometimes-cosmic leap to high school—is without a doubt the period in which all these study skills should be mastered, since doing so will make high school not just easier but a far more positive and successful experience.

If you're a "traditional" college student...

...somewhere in the 18 to 25 age range, I hope you are tackling one or two of the study skills you failed to master in high school (in which case I highly recommend you also study the appropriate other books in my *How to Study Program*). Otherwise, I can't see how you're ever going to succeed in college (then again, I can't conceive of how you managed to get *into* college). If you are starting from scratch, my advice is the same as to the high school students reading this book: Drop everything and make it your number one priority. Do not pass "Go." Do not order pizza.

If you're the parent of a student of any age

Your child's school is probably doing little if anything to teach him or her how to study. Which means he or she is not learning how to *learn*. And that means he or she is not learning how to *succeed*.

Should the schools be accomplishing that? Absolutely. After all, we spend $275 billion on elementary and secondary education in this country, *an average of $6,000 per student per year*. We ought to be getting more for that money than possible graduation, some football cheers, and an autographed yearbook.

What can parents do?

There are probably even more dedicated parents out there than dedicated students, because the first phone call at any of my radio or TV appearances usually comes from a sincere and worried parent asking, "What can I do to help my kid do better in school?" Okay, here they are, the rules for parents of students of any age:

1. **Set up a homework area.** Free of distraction, well-lit, all necessary supplies handy.
2. **Set up a homework routine.** When and where it gets done. Same time, same place, every day.
3. **Set homework priorities**. Make the point that homework *is* the priority—before a date, before TV, before going out to play, before whatever.
4. **Make reading a habit**—for them, certainly, but also for you, if it isn't already. Kids will inevitably

do what you *do*, not what you *say* (even if you say *not* to do what you *do*). So if you keep nagging them to read while you tune in for a 24-hour *Gilligan's Island* marathon, what message do you think you're giving them?

5. **Turn off the television.** Or, at the very least, severely limit when and how much TV-watching is appropriate.

6. **Talk to the teachers.** Find out what your kids are supposed to be learning. How else will you know what help they need? You may even be "helping" them in ways that are at odds with what the teacher is trying to accomplish.

7. **Encourage and motivate**, but don't nag them to do their homework. It doesn't work.

8. **Supervise their work**, but don't fall into the trap of *doing* their homework for them.

9. **Praise them to succeed**, but don't overpraise them for mediocre work. A sometimes misguided "self-esteem" movement has led to horrific grade inflation in the last decade. Kids are getting A's when they should be getting B's...or C's. Kids who should be forced to repeat a grade are getting promoted. Kids who need help—from you and their teachers—are getting the impression they're doing just fine, even if they are learning nothing at all.

10. **Convince older students of reality.** Learning and believing that the real world won't care about their grades, but measure them solely by what they know and what they can do, is a lesson that will save many tears (probably yours). It's probably never too early to tenderly inform your little genius that life really isn't fair...and give him or her the resources to deal with that fact.

11. **If you can afford it, get your kid(s) a computer** and all the software they can handle. Your kids, whatever their age, absolutely must master technology (computers) in order to survive, let alone succeed, in and after school.

12. **Turn off the TV already!**

13. **Get wired.** The Internet is the greatest invention of our age and an unbelievable tool for students of any age. While it's impossible to list even a smattering of helpful sites in a book this brief, parents of elementary and high school students should start by checking out:

    www.schoolwork.org

    www.sunsite.berkeley.edu/KidsClick

    www.HomeworkCentral.com
       (a division of *www.bigchalk.com*)

    www.iln.net

    www.tutor.com

The importance of your involvement

Don't for a minute underestimate the importance of *your* commitment to your child's success: Your involvement in your child's education is absolutely essential to his or her eventual success. The results of every study done in the last three decades clearly confirm the single factor that overwhelmingly affects a student's success in school: your involvement. Not money, great teachers, a bigger gym, or weekly dance classes. *You.*

So please, take the time to read this book (and all of the others in the series). Learn what your kids *should* be learning (and which of the other subject-specific books in the series your child needs the most).

And you can help tremendously, *even if you were not a great student yourself, even if you never learned great study skills.* You can learn now with your child—not only will it help him or her in school, it will help *you* on the job, whatever your field.

If you're a nontraditional student

If you're going back to high school, college, or graduate school at age 25, 45, 65, or 85—you probably need the help in *How to Study* more than anyone! Why? Because the longer you've been out of school, the more likely you don't remember what you've forgotten. And you've forgotten what you're supposed to remember! As much as I emphasize that it's rarely too early to learn good study habits, I must also emphasize that it's never too *late.*

What you won't find in *How to Study*

I've seen so-called study books spend chapters on proper nutrition, how to dress, how to exercise, and a number of other topics that are *not* covered *at all* in *How to Study,* except for this briefest of all acknowledgments: It is an absolute given that diet, sleep, exercise, and the use of drugs (including nicotine and caffeine) and alcohol all affect studying, perhaps significantly.

Having said that, I see little reason to waste your time detailing what should be obvious: Anything—including studying—is more difficult if you're tired, hungry, unhealthy, drunk, or stoned. So please use common sense. Eat as healthy as you can, get whatever sleep your body requires, stay reasonably fit, and avoid alcohol and drugs. If your lack of success is in any way due to one of these other factors and you're unable to deal with it alone, find a good book or a professional to help you.

Are you ready to learn something?

Learning shouldn't be painful or boring, though it is occasionally both. I don't promise that *How to Study* will make everything easier. It won't. It can't. And it may actually require some work to achieve what you want. But *How to Study will* show you the path, give you directions, and make sure you're properly provisioned for your journey.

You will not understand everything the first time you read it. Or, perhaps, even the second or third time. You may have to learn it slowly, very slowly. But that doesn't mean there's something wrong with you. It may be a subject that *everyone* learns slowly. (My particular nemesis was organic chemistry.)

You will also inevitably decide that one or more courses couldn't possibly be of any use later in life. "I don't have a clue why I'm busting my hump to learn this calculus (or algebra, physics, chemistry, European history, whatever)," you will lament. "I will *never* need it." Trust me, you have no idea what you may or may not need, use, or remember next *week,* let alone in a decade. I have found in my own life that a surprising amount of "useless" information and learning has been vitally important to my career.

So learn it all. Learn *more* than all. Get excited about the *process* of learning, and I guarantee you will not ever have to worry about what you will need to know in the future.

There are *other* study guides

Though I immodestly maintain my *How to Study Program* to be the most helpful to the most people, there are certainly lots of other purported study books out there. Unfortunately, I don't think many of them deliver what they promise. In fact, I'm actually getting mad at the growing number of study guides out there claiming to be "the sure way to straight A's" or something of the sort. These are also the books that dismiss reasonable alternative ways to study and learn with, "Well, that never worked for me," as if that is a valid reason to dismiss it, as if we should *care* that it didn't work for the author.

There are very few "rights" and "wrongs" out there in the study world. There's certainly no single "right" way to attack a multiple-choice test or absolute "right" way to take notes. So don't get fooled into thinking there *is*, especially if what you're doing seems to be working for you. Don't change what "ain't broke" just because some self-proclaimed study guru claims what you're doing is all wet. Maybe he's all wet.

Needless to say, don't read *my* books looking for the Truth—that single, inestimable system of "rules" that works for everyone. You won't find it, 'cause there's no such bird. You *will* find a plethora of techniques, tips, tricks, gimmicks, and what-have-you, some or all of which may work for you, some of which won't. Pick and choose, change and adapt, figure out what works for you. Because *you* are responsible for creating *your* study system, *not me*.

I think we've spent enough time talking about what you're *going* to learn. Let's get on with the learning.

—Ron Fry
May, 2000

How to Start Out Right

> " It is not enough to understand what we ought to be, unless we understand what we are; and we do not understand what we are, unless we know what we ought to be. "
>
> —T.S. Eliot

AKING A GOOD, honest look at yourself is not the easiest thing in the world to do. In the next two chapters, I'm going to help you evaluate the current level of all your study skills, a necessary step to identify the areas in which you need to concentrate your efforts; identify the study environment and learning style that suit you; and categorize all of your school subjects according to how well you *like* them and how well you *do* in them.

How to keep score

In the next few pages, I'll explain the 11 primary study skills covered in this book: reading and comprehension, memory development, time management, library skills, computer skills, textbook note-taking, classroom note-taking, library note-taking, classroom participation, paper-writing, and test preparation. Then I'll ask you to rate yourself on your current level of achievement and understanding of these skills: "A" for mastery or near mastery of a particular skill; "B" for some mastery; "C" for little or no mastery.

Remember: There are no right or wrong answers in this assessment. It's only a place to start, a jumping-off point from which you can measure your progress and rate those areas in which your skills need improvement.

To simplify the process, I've listed the primary study skills on page 20. Take a separate piece of paper and rate yourself on each of the 11 skills (from reading to test preparation) *before you read the rest of this chapter.* After you've rated yourself in each area, give yourself two points for every A, one point for every B, zero points for every C. If your overall rating is 18 or more, excellent (give yourself an A); 13 to 17, good (give yourself a B); and if 12 or less, fair (give yourself a C). Mark this rating under Initial Study Skills Evaluation.

Now, let's review each of these areas, giving you insight as to what "excellent," "good," and "fair" really mean. As you read each section, fill in your rating on the "Your Starting Point" chart—and be honest with yourself. This evaluation will give you a benchmark from which to measure your improvement after you've completed the book. File it away and compare your scores when you've completed this book.

Reading

Speed, comprehension, and recall are the three important components of reading. Comprehension and recall are especially interrelated—better to sacrifice some speed to increase these two factors. To test your reading and comprehension skills, read the passage on pages 20 through 22, close the book, and jot down the key points made in the selection you read, then review the text and compare your

Your Starting Point

Initial Study Skills Evaluation	A ☐	B ☐	C ☐
Reading	A ☐	B ☐	C ☐
Memory development	A ☐	B ☐	C ☐
Time management	A ☐	B ☐	C ☐
Textbook note-taking	A ☐	B ☐	C ☐
Classroom note-taking	A ☐	B ☐	C ☐
Classroom participation	A ☐	B ☐	C ☐
Basic library skills	A ☐	B ☐	C ☐
Computer skills	A ☐	B ☐	C ☐
Library note-taking	A ☐	B ☐	C ☐
Paper-writing	A ☐	B ☐	C ☐
Test preparation	A ☐	B ☐	C ☐
Overall study skills level	A ☐	B ☐	C ☐

notes with the reading selection. You will get a good idea of how well you understood what you read and just how effective your top-of-the-mind recall is.

The Brain

The brain is subdivided into four major areas. From the top down, you'll find: 1) the *cerebral cortex,* which I refer to as the cortex; 2) the *midbrain,* which contains a lot of the switching areas where nerves that pass up from below go to and from the cortex; 3) the *brainstem,* where much of the basic nervous system controls sit (coma occurs when this malfunctions, and death occurs when it is severed); and 4) the *cerebellum,* which sits behind the upper part of the brainstem and has traditionally been thought to regulate coordination of complex movements.

The cerebral cortex is the most newly evolved region of the brain and it is the part that separates humans from all the other mammals, especially the area in the front, appropriately named the *frontal cortex.* This area acts as a bridge between the sensory and motor circuits of the rest of the cortex and the older, deeper structures of the limbic system, which regulate drive and emotion. The frontal cortex is probably where much of our complex and abstract thoughts occur. It is probably where we put today in context with yesterday and tomorrow. When the frontal lobe is damaged, we become either more reactive and hypersexual like wild animals (without the step of logic in between to stop us) or very docile and unconcerned.

Behind the frontal cortex are the sensory and motor regions of the cortex, each divided up to correspond with specific areas on the opposite side of the body. Along the side are two protruding horns of cortex called the *temporal lobes.* Here, much of the processing of sound and verbal information occurs. Inside sits a deeper part of the limbic system called the *hippocampus.* The hippocampus acts like a way-station that coordinates the placement of information as it moves from sensory input to other areas of the brain.

In the back is the *occipital cortex,* where much of the processing of visual information occurs. The remaining areas along the side above the temporal horns form the *parietal cortex.* These areas are thought to be where a lot of cross-connection between the different sensory structures occurs. When the right side of the parietal cortex is damaged, very bizarre perceptions and reactions occur, such as ignoring one side of your body because you think it is a stranger.

The limbic system consists of the hippocampus, the rim of cortex on the inside of the halves around the corpus callosum called the *cingulate cortex*, and two almond-shaped heads near the frontal region, each one called the *amygdala*. This set of structures is the closest thing to what Freud referred to as the id, the seat of emotion and animal drive. It is the older region of the cortex in terms of evolution and is also involved in memory.

Strange things can happen when the cortex is damaged. (A great book on this subject is *The Man Who Mistook His Wife for a Hat,* by Dr. Oliver Sacks.) I find this particularly fascinating because it means that who you are as a person in terms of identity and interaction with other people depends completely on the complex and precise interaction of all these neural areas. It suggests that your identity depends on your neurology and not merely on a spirit living in your body.

Score: If you can read the material straight through and accurately summarize what you've read, all in less than two minutes, give yourself an A. If you have some problems reading and understanding the text but are able to complete the assignment in less than four minutes, give yourself a B. If you are unable to complete the assignment in that time, remember what you read, or produce accurate notes at all, give yourself a C.

Retention

There are specific methods to help you recall when you must remember a lot of specific facts. One of these is memorization—committing information to word-for-word recall. Memorize only when you are required to remember something for a relatively short time.

Test #1

Look at the number following this paragraph for 10 seconds. Then cover the page and write down as much of it as you can remember:

762049582049736

Test #2

Below are 12 nonsense words from a language I just made up and their "definitions." Study the list for 60 seconds in an attempt to remember each word, how it's spelled, and its definition:

pooted	tired	**nin**	hospital
ratoe	write	**mipp**	birthday
cout	child	**lermin**	car
whapple	swim	**chidder**	mouse
griven	zoo	**faib**	walk
carber	water	**zook**	dinner

Done? Close the book and write down each of the 12 words and its definition. They do not need to be in the order in which they were listed.

Score

Test # 1: If you remembered 12 or more digits in the correct order, give yourself an A; eight to 12, a B; seven or less, a C.

Test # 2: If you accurately listed eight or more words and definitions (and that includes spelling my new words correctly), give yourself an A. If you listed from five to seven words and their definitions, or correctly listed and spelled more than eight words but mixed up their definitions, give yourself a B. If you were unable to do either, give yourself a C.

Time management

Your effective use of available study time can be measured by two yardsticks: (1) your ability to break down assignments into component parts (for example, reading, note-taking, outlining, writing); and (2) your ability to complete each task in an efficient manner.

Score: If you feel you use your time wisely and efficiently, give yourself an A. If you know there are times you simply run out of time, give yourself a B. If you can't *tell* time, give yourself a C.

Library skills

Making the most of the library is a function of understanding its organization—and *using* it! The more time you spend there—studying, reading, researching—the more productive you'll be. You'll become adept at tracking down reference materials and finding the information you need quickly.

Virtually all libraries follow the same organization—once you understand it you'll be "library literate," no matter which library you use. In this book, you'll discover what kinds of resources are available (books, periodicals, directories, encyclopedias, dictionaries, magazines, newspapers, documents, microfilm files) and you'll learn how to find books (learning the Dewey Decimal and Library of Congress systems as well as using the library's computerized system).

To better evaluate your library skills, answer the following questions:

1. What collections are restricted in your library?

2. Where would you find a biography of Herbert Hoover in your local library?

3. Where is the reference section in your local library?

4. Given the Dewey number for a book, could you find it in less than five minutes? The Library of Congress number?

5. How often have you been to the library in the past six months? The past month?

6. Do you know how to find books, periodicals, and so forth using the library's computerized card catalog?

Score: If the answers to these questions are all obvious to you, indicating a steady pattern of library use, then you can claim to have the library habit—give yourself an A. If you can't answer one or more of the questions or will freely own up to a spotty record of library use, give yourself a B. If you don't have the faintest clue of where the closest library is, give yourself a C.

Computer skills

It's virtually impossible now to succeed at almost any level of education without complete mastery of the computer. But knowing how to use a computer, modem, and scanner is just the beginning. You have to know how to use them to study both more efficiently and effectively. That includes learning how to write better papers and keep your schedules and taking advantage of the almost limitless research possibilities available online.

Score: If you are capable of doing just about anything online short of hacking the Pentagon and have made your computer equipment a key tool in your quest for more efficient studying and better grades, give yourself an A. If you are adept at word processing and playing games and at least can get online, but have never used 75 percent of the other tools on your computer and "wipe out" more often than surf, give yourself a B. If you don't even know what "being online" means and need four minutes to figure out how to turn your computer on, give yourself a C.

Note-taking

Three different arenas—at home with your textbooks, in the classroom, and at the library—require different methods of note-taking.

From your textbooks: Working from your books at home, you should identify the main ideas, rephrasing information in your own words, as well as capturing the details with which you are unfamiliar. Take brief, concise notes in a separate notebook as you read. You should write down questions and answers to ensure your mastery of the material, starring those questions to which you *don't* have answers so you can ask them in class.

In class: Class *preparation* is the key to class *participation.* By reading material to be covered before class, you will be able to concentrate and absorb the teacher's interpretations and points. Using a topical, short sentence approach or your own shorthand or symbols, take notes on those items that will trigger thematic comprehension of the subject matter. Your notes should be sequential, following the teacher's lecture pattern. Review your notes at the first opportunity following class. Fill in any blanks and your own thoughts.

In the library: What's the difference between taking notes at the library or working at home with library books vs. your own textbooks? Sooner or later you'll have to return library books (if you're allowed to take them out at all), and librarians tend to frown on highlighting them, so you need an effective system for library note-taking. In Chapter 6, I'll show you mine.

Score: If you feel that your note-taking skills are sufficient to summarize the necessary data from your textbooks and capture the key points from classroom lectures and discussions and they allow you to prepare detailed outlines and write good papers, give yourself an A. If you feel any one of these three areas is deficient, give yourself a B. If notes are what you pass to your friends in class, give yourself a C.

Class participation

In my experience, there are few teachers who don't take each student's class participation into account when giving grades, no matter how many pop quizzes they pull or how many term papers they assign. And, you may have discovered, there are teachers out there who will mark down students who "ace" every paper and quiz if they habitually disappear in the classroom.

Score: If you are always prepared for class (which means, at the very least, reading all assigned material, preparing assigned homework and projects, and turning them in on time), actively participate in discussions, and ask frequent and pertinent questions as a way of both trumpeting what you already know and filling in the gaps in that knowledge, give yourself an A. If you fail in any of these criteria, give yourself a B. If you aren't sure where the classroom is, give yourself a C.

Paper-writing

Preparing any sort of report, written or oral, is 90 percent perspiration (research) and 10 percent inspiration (writing). In other words, the ability to write a good paper is more dependent on your mastery of the other skills we've already discussed than your mastery of _writing_. If you are an avid reader, familiar with your local library, a good note-taker, and capable of breaking down the most complex topic into the manageable steps necessary to write a paper, you probably turn in superior papers.

Score: If you have already given yourself an A in library skills, library note-taking, time management, and reading, give yourself an A. If you feel you turn in relatively good papers but definitely underperform in any of these areas, give yourself a B. If your idea of writing a paper is photocopying the pertinent Cliffs Notes and recopying the summary in your own handwriting, give yourself a C.

Test preparation

The key to proper test preparation is an accurate assessment of what material will be covered and what form the test will take. Weekly quizzes or unit/chapter exams usually cover the most recent material. Midterms and finals cover a much broader area—usually all the subject matter to date. Multiple-choice tests, essays, lists of math problems, and science lab tests all require different preparation and applying different test-taking skills. Knowing the kind of test you're facing will make your preparation much easier.

So will creating a list of questions you think your teacher will most likely ask. Through periodic review of your text and class notes, the areas in which your teacher appears most interested—and on which he or she is most likely to test you—should begin to emerge. As a final trick, prepare a list of 10 or more questions *you* would ask if *you* were the teacher.

Score: If you are able to construct tests that are harder than the ones your teacher gives you—and you perform well on those—give yourself an A. If you feel you know the material, but somehow don't perform as well as you think you should at test time, give yourself a B. If you didn't pass your driver's test, let alone algebra, give yourself a C.

Your overall score

Once again, after you've rated yourself in each area, give yourself two points for every A, one point for every B, zero points for every C. If your overall rating is 18 or more, excellent (give yourself an A); 13 to 17, good (give yourself a B); and if 12 or less, fair (give yourself a C). Put your new score in the section "Overall study skills level" in the chart on page 20.

Now what?

The fact that you have been honest with yourself in evaluating those talents you bring into the study game is a big plus in your favor. Knowing where you are strong and where you need to improve makes everything else a good deal easier. Now, based on your test results, draw up a list of your assets and liabilities—your areas of strength and weakness. This will focus your attention on those areas that will require the most work to improve.

While I would strongly recommend you read the entire book, this simple test has enabled you to identify the chapters you really need to work on and the specific skills that may require work long after you finish reading this book.

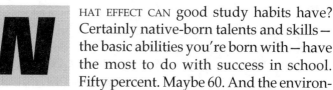

CHAPTER 2

How to Organize Your Studying

WHAT EFFECT CAN good study habits have? Certainly native-born talents and skills — the basic abilities you're born with — have the most to do with success in school. Fifty percent. Maybe 60. And the environment in which you're trying to learn, your health, and other such factors may be another 10 percent, maybe 15. That leaves 25 to 40 percent for study skills.

Don't believe that learning how to study can have such a monstrous effect? Two comments: One, try me. Read *How to Study*, practice the skills, watch the results. I think you'll discover I'm right. Second, if you don't believe study skills are so important, you must be giving more weight to ability, kind of a "smart kids do well because they're smart" approach. Well, a lot of smart kids *don't* do well. *At all*.

Others do well in school but test poorly. And many are great in some subjects and not so great in others. I don't have to prove this. Look at your friends, at others in your school. I guarantee you'll prove it to yourself.

What kind of effort are we talking about here? Another hour a night? Two hours a night? *More?* And what about that "study smarter, not harder" slogan that's plastered all over the bookstore display for the *How to Study Program.* "If I'm studying longer," you might reasonably contend, "I'm sure as heck studying harder, at least by my definition."

Let's take the latter point first. You *can* study smarter. You *can* put in less time and get better results. But learning how to do so *is* hard, because learning of *any* kind takes discipline. And learning self-discipline is, to many of us, the most difficult task of all. So don't kid yourself: You aren't going to sit down, read *How to Study*, and miraculously transform yourself from a C-student into an A-student. But you absolutely can do so if you put in the time to learn the lessons *Study* contains and, more importantly, practice and use them every day.

If you're currently doing little or nothing in the way of schoolwork, then you *are* going to have to put in more time and effort. How much more? Or even more generally, how long should you study, period? Until you get the results you want to achieve. The smarter you are and the more easily you learn and adapt the techniques in *How to Study*, the more likely you will be spending less time on your homework than before. But the further you need to go—from D's to A's rather than B's to A's—the more you need to learn and the longer you need to give yourself to learn it.

Don't get discouraged. You will see results surprisingly quickly.

Make study habit-forming

If you're doing poorly in school and you're actually putting in a reasonable amount of study time, you've got poor study habits. Who knows where or when you acquired them, but failure has, to some extent, become a habit.

Good news! Not only can *bad* habits be broken, but they can be replaced by *good* habits relatively easily. Here's your battle plan:

✎ It is much easier to *replace* one of your habits than to break it entirely. So don't attempt to stop poor study habits, just learn the good ones that substitute for them.

✎ Practice, practice, practice. There's no way around it: Practice is the motor oil that lubricates any habit's engine. The more you do something, the more ingrained it becomes. Just ask any smoker — if you can still find one — how many times he lit a cigarette just today without even noticing that he had done so!

✎ Tell your friends and family of your decision to do better in school by honing your study skills. This is a trick that works for *some* people, who find that the added pressure is a good motivator.

Smokers are notorious for doing this, hoping that the fear of embarrassment (of disappointing all those friends and family if they light up again) will serve as one more strong motivation to quit. For some of you, however, such a strategy simply adds *too much* pressure and is more likely to backfire instead, encouraging *failure.* My advice would be to use such a strategy if you know it will help you personally, but to avoid it if you know it will actually hurt.

✎ You don't have to grind it out from D's to A's with no feedback. Obviously, there's a lot of distance you're traveling and you'll be seeing the effects of better study habits all along the way. And each effect you see just strengthens your resolve and makes it even easier to keep on going. To make sure you get a "motivational jolt" from every accomplishment, resolve to chart every inch of your progress, even if, like Robert Frost, you have miles to go before you sleep. You may want to set up a chart on your wall on which you list "Today's Successes" *every day*. And remember the small steps you're taking—saving five minutes on a reading assignment, finding the books you need at the library more quickly, feeling that you took good notes in a lecture, raising your hand to actually answer a professor's question in a class discussion, and so on.

Starting with the next chapter, everything in this book will concentrate on specific strategies useful for specific tasks—paper-writing, note-taking, test-taking, reading, and so forth. So this is probably the best place to discuss some overall study strategies that have little to do with any particular task and everything to do with achieving overall study success.

Get ready to become a "lifer"

Learning how to study is really a long-term process. Once you undertake the journey, you will be surprised at the number of landmarks, pathways, side streets, and road signs you'll find. Even after you've transformed yourself into a better student than you'd ever hoped to be, you'll inevitably find one more signpost that offers new information, one more pathway that leads you in an interesting new direction. Consider learning how to study a *lifelong process* and be ready to modify anything you're doing as you learn another method.

This is especially important right from the start when you consider your overall study strategies. How long you study per night, how long you work on a particular subject and how often you schedule breaks are going to vary considerably depending on how well you were doing before you read this book, how far you have to go, how interested you are in getting there, how involved you are in other activities, the time of day, your general health — are you getting the idea?

It gets more complicated: What's your study strategy? Your high school history teacher may want you to memorize a series of battles, dates, and generals. Your college professor will expect a deeper understanding of the battles, how they related to the overall conduct of the war, and how they affected or were affected by what was occurring in the rest of the world. *Your teacher's emphasis will change the way you study.* What's your study sequence? Hardest assignments first? Easiest? Longest? Shortest? Are you comfortable switching back and forth from one to another or do you need to focus on a single assignment from start to finish?

This gets even more difficult (believe it or not!) when you consider that the tasks themselves may have a great effect on your schedule. When I sit down to plan out the chapter of a book, for example, I need a relatively long period of uninterrupted time — at least an hour, perhaps as long as three hours — in order to get my notes in the order I want them and to think through the entire chapter, writing transitions in my head, noting problem areas, figuring out where I need an example or illustration. If I only have half an hour before a meeting or appointment, I wouldn't even attempt to start such a project, since I'd just have to start all over again when I had the right amount of time.

You may find yourself to be the same way and, therefore, need to ensure your schedule is flexible enough to adapt to the demands of the specific task. Fifteen-minute study unit increments might work well for you most of the time (though I suspect half an hour is an ideal unit for most of you, an hour only for those of you who can work that long without a break and who have assignments that traditionally take that long to complete).

On the other hand, you may have no problem at all working on a long project in fits and starts, 15 or 20 minutes at a time, without needing to retrace your steps each time you pick it up again.

What's the lesson in all of this? There is no ideal, no answer—certainly no "right" answer—to many of the questions I've posed. It's a message you'll read in these pages over and over again: Figure out what works for you and keep on doing it. If it later stops working or doesn't seem to be working as well, change it.

None of the study techniques discussed at such length in this book is carved in stone. You not only should feel free to adapt and shape and bend them to your own needs, you *must* do so.

Follow the Yellow Brick Road

When I talk about test-taking, one of the key bits of advice is to read the instructions before you start the test. This helps you avoid the poor grade (not to mention the frustration and embarrassment) that results from trying to answer all six essay questions in an hour when you were only supposed to pick three.

Tests aren't the only time when reading the instructions is important. Many teachers have their own rules and regulations about turning in homework assignments, preparing papers or projects, reporting lab results, and so forth. And it's just as important to follow these instructions—and just as devastating if you *don't*.

I really did have a teacher in high school—when none of us had access to personal computers and few of us had learned to type—who failed a student because her paper was handwritten. What bothered me then was that the paper was really *good*...and it didn't mean a hill of beans to that teacher. Isn't it ridiculous to get a low grade for such a lousy reason?

Be proud of your work...and show it

Do you know any students who make sure they count every word on their 500-word assignment and head to a conclusion as soon as they reach that magic number?

How about the student who is convinced his chicken scratch is perfectly decipherable, even when the teacher has to wade through several cross-outs on every page and follow arrows from one page to another because the student thought the order should be changed after the fact?

Or those who only spell one thing correctly per paper— their name—or, even worse, spell a word correctly two or three times and incorrectly four or five others, all on the same page?

Teachers are human. They respond to presentation. While I am not advocating—and most teachers will not buy—an emphasis on form over substance, one should certainly consider that if the substance of two papers or tests or projects is relatively equal, the form in which they're presented may well affect the grade, perhaps significantly.

Besides, there are a lot of teachers who make it a point to decrease grades because of poor grammar, spelling, presentation. (And others who may subconsciously increase grades—or give a better grade than the work really warrants—because the presentation was done with care and a sense of pride.)

Know thy teachers

Teachers are different, too, in their approach to their subjects, as well as their expectations, standards, flexibility, and so on. It certainly is worth the effort to compile a "profile" of each of your teachers. What does each of them want to see in terms of notes, level of participation, papers, projects? What are their individual likes and dislikes? Their methods of grading and testing?

Knowing these various traits should certainly lead you to some adaptation of your approach to each class. Let's say—not that it would ever _really_ happen to _you_, of course—that you have managed to dig yourself a very deep hole. It's 11 p.m., you're well past your study prime, and you still have reading assignments to complete for English and history tomorrow morning.

Your English teacher demands maximum class participation and makes it a large part of your grade—and your test scores be damned. Her hobby seems to be calling on the unprepared, and she has an uncanny and unerring knack for ferreting those students out.

Your history teacher discourages discussion, preferring to lecture and answer a couple of questions at the end of the class. He never calls on anyone for anything. Given this situation, and knowing you can stay awake long enough to read only one of the two assignments, which would it be?

In fact, presuming you care at all about your studies and grades, would there _ever_ be a time, barring a simultaneous typhoon, eclipse, and national holiday, that you would show up for that English class unprepared?

While I'll show you in Chapter 4 how to ensure that poor scheduling does not become a habit that leads to such choices, I suspect far too many of you do not take the natural differences among your various teachers into account when scheduling homework, preparing papers, or studying for tests.

Likewise, I suspect far too few of you try to create a bond with one special teacher—a mentoring relationship—that could well help you avoid some of the bumps and swerves and help you reach your goal with far less trouble. Why should you go out of your way to find a mentor? Because you probably need more help — in life, not just in school — than your friends or parents can provide. A mentor can give you that perspective, advice, and help.

Intrinsic and extrinsic motivation

Motivators are either intrinsic or extrinsic. What's the difference? You sign up for a voice class. While the hours certainly apply to your graduating requirements, you attend class because you love singing.

You also signed up for biology. You hate the thought of dissecting frogs, and you couldn't care less whether they have exoskeletons, endoskeletons, hydroskeletons, or no skeletons at all, but the class is required.

In the first case, you're motivated by *intrinsic* factors — you are taking the voice class simply because you truly enjoy it.

The second scenario is an example of *extrinsic* motivation. While you have no interest in biology, your reward for taking the class is external — you'll be able to graduate.

Extrinsic motivation can help you make it through boring or unpleasant tasks that are part of the process of reaching your goals. A vivid image of your final goal can be a powerful motivating force. One student thought about what his job as a computer programmer would be like whenever he needed some help getting through class.

Try imagining what a day in *your* life will be like five or 10 years down the road. If you haven't the faintest clue, no *wonder* you're having a hard time motivating yourself to work toward that career as a final goal!

A specific role model may also be an effective motivator. When she was a first grader, my daughter Lindsay became particularly enamored of Wilma Rudolph. Growing up black and poor was a minor part of Wilma's childhood problems. When she contracted polio, doctors told her she would never walk again. My daughter thought it was amazing that Wilma, through sheer guts and determination, not only walked again but became the fastest woman in the world, winning multiple Olympic gold medals. When confronted with her own (smaller!) problems, my daughter still reminds herself that "if Wilma could do it, I can, too." What a great way to motivate yourself! Think of your own role models in life. And if you don't have any, find some!

The goal pyramid

One way to easily visualize all your goals—and their relation to each other—is to construct what I call a *goal pyramid*. Here's how to do it:

1. Centered at the top of a piece of paper, write down what you hope to ultimately gain from your education. This is your long-range goal and the pinnacle of your pyramid. For example, let's say you want to become a successful advertising copywriter.

2. Below your long-range goal(s), list mid-range goals—milestones or steps that will lead you to your eventual target. For example, if your long-range goal were to become an advertising copywriter, your mid-range goals might include getting into college, doing well in all your writing courses, completing all required courses, and getting a summer internship at a major ad agency.

3. Below the mid-range goals, list as many short-range goals as you can—smaller steps that can be completed in a relatively short period of time. For example, if your long-range goal is to become an advertising copywriter, your short-range

goals may include taking copywriting or advertising courses.

Change your goal pyramid as you progress through school. You may eventually decide on a different career. Or your mid-range goals may change as you decide on a different path leading to the long-range goal. The short-range goals will undoubtedly change, maybe even daily.

The process of creating your own goal pyramid allows you to see *how* all those little daily and weekly steps you take can lead to your mid-range and long-term goals, and will thereby motivate you to work on your daily and weekly tasks with more energy and enthusiasm.

Make goal-setting a part of your life

The development of good study skills is the highway to your goals, whatever they are. And no matter how hard you have to work or how much adversity you have to overcome along the way, the journey will indeed be worth it.

How do you make setting goals a part of your life? Here are some hints I think will help:

1. **Be realistic when you set goals.** Don't aim too high (or too low) and don't be particularly concerned when — not if — you have to make adjustments along the way.

2. **Be realistic about your expectations.** You may *never* master calculus or physics, so don't get discouraged if you can't. But *do* attempt to do the best you can. A "B" or even a "C" may well *be* the best *you* can do in a particularly difficult subject.

3. **Don't give up too easily.** You can be *overly* realistic — too ready to give up because something

is a trifle harder than you'd like. Don't aim too high and feel miserable when you don't come close, or aim too low and never achieve your potential—find the path that's right for you.

4. **Concentrate on areas that offer the best chance for improvement.** Unexpected successes can do wonders for your confidence and might make it possible for you to achieve more than you thought you could even in other areas.

5. **Monitor your achievements and keep resetting your goals.** Daily, weekly, monthly, yearly—ask yourself how you've done and where you'd like to go *now*.

Use rewards as artificial motivators

The way you decide to use a reward system all depends on how much help you need getting motivated to study. As we've observed, tasks that are intrinsically interesting require little outside motivation. However, most schoolwork can be spurred along by the promise of little rewards along the way. If the task is especially tedious or difficult, make the rewards more frequent so that motivation doesn't sag.

As a general rule, the size of the reward should match the difficulty of the task. For an hour of reading, promise yourself a 10-minute walk. For completion of a rough draft for a big assignment, treat yourself to a movie.

3 great ways to get super-organized

As you begin to make goal-setting and organization a part of your daily life, here are three concepts that will make a huge difference in your success.

Small changes, over time, make a big difference

A simple, tiny change in your behavior may have virtually negligible results, but make *hundreds* of small changes, and the effects can be earth-shattering!

Make this rule become an automatic part of your thought process and your actions. It will help you understand the often small difference between success and failure, productivity and frustration, happiness and agony. It's so simple, it's deceptive. Maybe just a little more training. Maybe a slightly better method of planning. Maybe just one tiny habit overcome. Maybe all of these and more. Each one alone is almost inconsequential, but when added up, the advantage is incredible!

The 80-20 Rule (Pareto Principle)

Another rule that you can apply to make a difference in how well you organize and manage your priorities is the 80-20 Rule, also known as the Pareto Principle.

Victor Pareto was an Italian economist and sociologist who studied land ownership in Italy at the turn of the 20th century. Pareto discovered that more than 80 percent of all the land was owned by less than 20 percent of the people. As he studied other things that people owned (including money), he found the same principle held true: 20 percent or less of the people always ended up with 80 percent or more of whatever he measured.

The most astonishing revelation about the 80-20 Rule is its opposite side: If 20 percent of activities are producing 80 percent of the results, then the other 80 percent of activities are, in total, only giving 20 percent of the results.

Remember: To apply the 80-20 Rule to managing your priorities, remind yourself that 20 percent of the activities on your list are going to produce 80 percent of the results and payoff. Your question must constantly be, "Which activities are the 20-percenters?"

Take advantage of "in-between" time

You can be even more productive by identifying the little windows of opportunity that pass through your life each day. They don't arrive with much fanfare, so if you're not alert to them, they will sneak right past you. What must you do with this "in-between" time? Recognize it as soon as it occurs and utilize it immediately by taking a premeditated action. If you don't have a plan, you will waste this time!

Here are some suggestions:

✎ Make phone calls.

✎ Read something.

✎ Mail letters.

✎ Pick up groceries (or make your grocery list).

✎ Clean your desk and return things to their proper places.

✎ Review your Daily Schedule and reprioritize, if necessary.

✎ Go through your mail.

✎ Write a quick note or letter home.

✎ Proofread some or all of one of your papers.

✎ Think! (About an upcoming assignment, a paper you're writing, any upcoming project.)

✎ Relax!

How perfect are you?

Remember our earlier discussion about "showing you care" and taking the time to "do things right"? Perfectionists care perhaps too much, finding it impossible to be satisfied with anything less than "perfect" work (as they define it), presuming for a moment that such an ideal can actually be attained.

It is possible, of course, to score a "perfect" 100 on a test or to get an A+ on a paper the teacher calls "Perfect!" in the margin. But in reality, doing anything "perfectly" is an impossible task.

What does all this have to do with you? Nothing, unless you find yourself spending two hours polishing an already A+ paper or half an hour searching for that one "perfect" word or an hour rewriting great notes to make them "absolutely perfect." In other words, while striving for perfection may well be a noble trait, it can very easily, perhaps inevitably, become a major problem if it becomes an uncontrollable and unstoppable urge.

If you find yourself fighting this demon, remind yourself (frequently) of the Law of Diminishing Returns: Your initial effort yields the biggest results, with each succeeding effort yielding proportionately less. And there comes a point when even the most *prodigious* efforts yield *negligible* results. This applies not only to perfectionists, but also to those of you who scoff at the very thought of using a "simple" outline or producing a "formulaic" report. You do not have to always be innovative, dazzling, and creative. You do not have to invent a new, multimedia, interactive book report. Sometimes a good six-page book report that gets an A- is just fine, and that A+ "innovation" is more trouble (and time!) than it's worth!

When I am tempted to do far more than necessary, just because it would be a "cool" solution (and time consuming and wasteful and inefficient and difficult), I think of George Simenon, the French author best known for his Inspector Maigret mystery series — and the *500 total books he wrote* in his lifetime. How did he do it...and still have time to eat and sleep? Simple. He used only 2,000 vocabulary words (out of the 800,000 plus available to him) so he wouldn't have to interrupt his writing to consult a dictionary or thesaurus. (And he probably didn't eat or sleep much either.)

If you are perfectionistic — a little or a whole lot — recognize that trait and take the necessary steps to rein it in when you want (or need) to. If you really would prefer spending another couple of hours polishing that A+ paper or searching for a Web site your teacher's never heard of to taking in a movie, reading a book, or getting some *other* assignment done, be my guest. Is the extra effort *really* worth it? Probably not.

Creating *your* study environment

On page 46, I have included a checklist for you to rate your study environment. It includes not just *where* you study — at home, in the library, at a friend's house — but *when* and *how* you study, too. Once you've identified what works for you, avoid those situations in which you *know* you don't perform best. If you don't know the answer to one or more of the questions, take the time to experiment.

(For more information about creating the ideal study environment, be sure to read **Get Organized**, another of the books in my **How to Study Program**.)

Many of the items on this chart should be understandable to you now. *Why* you feel the need for a particular environment is not important. Knowing you *have a preference* is. Here's what you're trying to assess in each item:

1. If you prefer "listening" to "seeing," you'll have little problem getting the information you need from class lectures and discussion. In fact, you'll *prefer* them to studying your textbooks. (You may have to concentrate on your reading skills and spend more time with your textbooks to offset this tendency. Highlighting your texts may help.)

My Ideal Study Environment

How I receive information best:
1. ❏ Orally ❏ Visually

In the classroom, I should:
2. ❏ Concentrate on taking notes
   ❏ Concentrate on listening

3. ❏ Sit in front ❏ Sit in back
   ❏ Sit near window or door

Where I study best:
4. ❏ At home ❏ In the library
   ❏ Somewhere else:_____

When I study best:
5. ❏ Every night; little on weekends
   ❏ Mainly on weekends
   ❏ Spread out over seven days

6. ❏ In the morning ❏ Evening ❏ Afternoon

7. ❏ Before dinner ❏ After dinner

How I study best:
8. ❏ Alone ❏ With a friend ❏ In a group

9. ❏ Under time pressure ❏ Before I know I have to

10. ❏ With music ❏ In front of TV ❏ In a quiet room

11. ❏ Organizing an entire night's studying before I start
    ❏ Tackling and completing one subject at a time

I need to take a break:
12. ❏ Every 30 minutes or so ❏ Every hour
    ❏ Every 2 hours ❏ Every _____ hours

If you're more of a "visual" person, you'll probably find it easier reading your textbook and may have to work to improve your classroom concentration. Taking excellent class notes that you can read later will probably be important for you. You'll also want to adapt your note-taking methods to your visual preference — rather than writing notes like everybody else, draw pictures, use charts, and learn how to "map" a lecture. (See Chapters 5 and 7 for a complete discussion of note-taking techniques.)

2. This should tie in with your answer to (1). The more "aural" you are, the more you should concentrate on listening. The more "visual," the better your notes should be for later review.

3. This may make a difference for a number of reasons. You may find it difficult to hear or see from the back of the classroom. You may be shy and want to sit up front to motivate yourself to participate in class discussions. You may find sitting near a window makes you feel a little less claustrophobic; alternatively, you may daydream too much if near a window and should sit as far "inside" the classroom as possible.

4. Whatever location you find most conducive to study (considering the limitations of your current living situation and schedule) should be where you spend most of your study time.

5. How to organize your time to most effectively cover the material: This may depend, in part, on the amount of homework you are burdened with and/or the time of year. You may have one schedule during most of the school year but have to adapt during test time, if papers are due, for special projects, and so on.

6. To some of you, such preferences may only be a factor on weekends, because your day hours are set—you're in school.

    But if you're in college (or in a high school program that mimics college's "choose your own courses and times" scheduling procedures), you would want to use this factor in determining when to schedule your classes.

    If you study best in the morning, for example, try to schedule as many classes as possible in the afternoons (or, at worst, late in the morning).

    If you study best in the evening, either schedule morning classes and leave your afternoons free for other activities, or schedule them in the afternoons so you can sleep later (and study later the night before).

7. Some of us get cranky if we try to do *anything* when we're hungry. If you study poorly when your stomach is growling, eat something!

8. Most of us grow up automatically studying alone. If we study with a friend, there's often more talking, TV watching, anything *but* studying than studying. But don't underestimate the positive effect studying with one or two friends—or even a larger study group—can have on your mastery of schoolwork and on your grades. (I discuss study groups in greater detail at the end of this section.)

9. Just because you perform best under pressure doesn't mean you should always leave projects, papers, and studying for tests until the last minute. It just means if you're well-organized, but an unexpected project gets assigned or a surprise test announced, you won't panic.

    If you do *not* study well under pressure, it certainly doesn't mean you occasionally won't be required to do so. The better organized you are, the easier it will be for you all the time, but especially when the unexpected arises.

10. As we've discussed, some of you (like me) will find it difficult to concentrate with*out* music or some sort of noise. Others couldn't sit in front of the TV and do *any*thing but breathe and eat. Many of you will fall in between—you can read and even take notes to music but need absolute quiet to study for a test or master particularly difficult concepts. If you don't know how you function best, now is the time to find out.

11. Back to organizing. The latter concept—starting and finishing one project before moving on to another—doesn't mean you can't at least sit down and outline an entire night's study plan before tackling each subject, one at a time. Setting up such a study schedule *is* advised. But it may mean you really *can't* move to another project while the one you're now working on is unfinished. Others of you may have no problem working on one project, switching to another when you get stuck or just need a break, then going back to the first.

12. There's nothing particularly wrong with taking a break whenever you feel you need to keep yourself sharp and maximize your quality study time—as long as the breaks aren't every five minutes and don't last longer than the study periods! In general, though, try to increase your concentration through practice so that you can go at least an hour before getting up, stretching, and having a drink or snack. Too many projects will require at least that long to "get into" or organize, and you may find that breaking too frequently will require too much "review time" when you return to your desk.

Study groups: What are friends for?

Surprisingly enough, I was 35 years old and a devoted watcher of the television show *The Paper Chase* before I was introduced to the concept of a study group. This series was supposed to be about a law school that seemed just this side of hell, so sharing the load with other students wasn't just a good idea, it was virtually mandatory for survival. My high school certainly wasn't hell, not even a mild purgatory, but I still think a study group would have been beneficial. If I had thought of the idea myself, even while I was in high school, I would have probably started one.

The idea is simple: Find a small group of like-minded students—four to six seems to be an optimal number—and share notes, question each other, prepare for tests together. To be effective, obviously, the students you pick to be in your group should share all, or at least most, of your classes. (In college, single-subject study groups are common.)

Search out students who are smarter than you, but not *too* much smarter. If they are on a level far beyond your own, you'll soon be left in the dust and be more discouraged than ever. On the other hand, if you choose students who are too far beneath your level, you may enjoy being the "brain" of the bunch but miss the point of the group—the challenge of other minds to spur you on.

Study groups can be organized in a variety of ways. Each member could be assigned primary responsibility for a single class, such as preparing detailed notes from lectures and discussion groups. If supplementary reading is recommended but not required, that person could be responsible for doing all such reading and preparing detailed summaries.

Alternatively, everybody can be responsible for his or her own notes, but the group could act as an *ad hoc* discussion group, refining understanding of key points, working on problems together, questioning each other, practicing for tests, and so forth.

Even if you find only one or two other students willing to work with you, such cooperation will be invaluable, especially in preparing for major exams.

Tips for forming your own study group

✎ I suggest four students minimum, probably six maximum. You want to ensure everyone gets a chance to participate as much as they want while maximizing the collective knowledge and wisdom of the group.

✎ While group members needn't be best friends, they shouldn't be overtly hostile to one another, either. Seek diversity of experience, demand common dedication.

✎ Try to select students who are at least as smart, committed, and serious as you. That will encourage you to keep up and challenge you a bit. Avoid a group in which you're the "star" — at least until you flicker out during the first exam.

✎ Avoid inviting members who are inherently unequal into the group — boyfriend/girlfriend combinations, in which one or the other may be inhibited by their *amore*'s presence; situations where one student works for another; situations where underclassmen and upperclassmen may stifle one another. You get the idea.

✎ Decide early on if you're forming a study group or a social group. If it's the latter, don't pretend it's the former. If the former, don't just invite your friends and informally sit around discussing your teachers for an hour each week.

✎ There are a number of ways to organize, as we briefly discussed previously. My suggestion is to assign each class to one student. That student must truly master that assigned class, doing, in addition to the regular assignments, of course: any or all additional reading (recommended by the professor or not) necessary to achieve that goal; taking outstanding notes; outlining the course (if the group decides that would be helpful); being available for questions about specific topics in the class; and preparing various practice quizzes, midterms, and finals, as needed, to help test the other students' mastery.

Needless to say, all of the other students still attend all classes, take their own notes, and do their own reading and homework assignments. But the student assigned that class attempts to learn as much as the professor, to actually *be* the "substitute professor" of that class in the study group. (So if you have five classes, a five-person study group is ideal.)

✎ Make meeting times and assignments formal and rigorous. Consider establishing rigid rules of conduct. For example, miss two meetings, whatever the excuse, and you're out. Better to shake out the nonserious students early. You don't want anyone who is working as little as possible but hoping to take advantage of *your* hard work.

✎ Consider appointing a chair (rotating weekly, if you wish) in charge of keeping everyone on schedule and settling disputes before they disrupt the study group.

✎ However you organize, clearly decide—early—the exact requirements and assignments of each student. Again, you never want the feeling to emerge that one or two of you are trying to "ride the coattails" of the others.

Where should *you* study?

At the library. There may be numerous choices, from the large reading room, to quieter, sometimes deserted specialty rooms, to your own study cubicle. My favorite "home away from home" at Princeton was a little room that seemingly only four or five of us knew about—with four wonderfully comfortable chairs, subdued lighting, phonographs with earplugs, and a selection of some 500 classical records. For someone who needed music to study, it was custom-made!

At home. Remember that this is the place where distractions are most likely to occur. No one tends to telephone you at the library, and little brothers (or your own kids) will not find you easily among the stacks of books. It is, of course, usually the most convenient place to make your study headquarters. It may not, however, be the most effective.

At a friend's, neighbor's, or relative's house. This may not be an option at all for most of you, even on an occasional basis, but you may want to set up one or two alternative study sites. Despite many experts' opinion that you must study in the same place every night (with which I don't necessarily agree), I had a friend who simply craved some variety to help motivate him. He had four different places he liked to study and rotated them from night to night. Do whatever works for you.

In an empty classroom. Certainly an option at many colleges and perhaps some private high schools, it is an interesting idea mainly because so few students have ever thought of it! While not a likely option at a public high school, it never hurts to ask if you can't make some arrangements. Since many athletic teams practice until 6 p.m. or later, even on the high school level, there may be a part of the school open—and usable with permission—even if the rest is locked up tight.

At your job. Whether you're a student working part-time or a full-timer going to school part-time, you may well be able to make arrangements to use an empty office, even during regular office hours, or perhaps after everyone has left (depending on how much your boss trusts you). If you're in junior high or high school and a parent, friend, or relative works nearby, you may be able to work from just after school until closing time at his or her workplace.

When should you study

As much as possible, create a routine time of day you study. Some students find it easier to set aside specific blocks of time during the day, each day, in which they plan on studying. The time of day you'll study is determined by these factors:

1. **Study when you're at your best.** What is your peak performance period — the time of day you do your best work? This period varies from person to person — you may be dead to the world until noon but able to study well into the night, or up and alert at the crack of dawn but distracted and tired if you try to burn the midnight oil.

2. **Consider your sleep habits.** Habit is a very powerful influence. If you always set your alarm for 7 a.m., you may find that you wake up then even when you forget to set it. If you have grown accustomed to going to sleep around 11 p.m., you will undoubtedly become quite tired if you try to stay up studying until 2 a.m., and probably accomplish very little in the three extra hours.

3. **Study when you can.** Although you want to sit down to study when you are mentally most

alert, external factors also play a role in deciding when you study. Being at your best is a great goal but not always possible. Study whenever circumstances allow.

4. **Consider the complexity of the assignment when you allocate time.** The tasks themselves may have a great effect on your schedule.

5. **Use "nonprime" hours for the easiest tasks.** When your energy and motivation are at their lowest levels, should you really bore in on that project that's been giving you fits? When you're least creative, least energetic, and least motivated, why would you even consider tackling your most challenging assignments? Don't be like many businesspeople I know who schedule their time "bass-ackwards": In the morning, when they're raring to go, they read the paper, check their e-mail, and skim trade journals. At the *end* of the day, when they can barely see straight, they start on the presentation for the Board of Directors' meeting...*tomorrow's* Board of Directors' meeting.

Evaluate your study area

Whatever location you choose as your study base, how you set up your study area can affect your ability to stay focused and, if you aren't careful, seriously inhibit quality study time. Sit down at your desk or study area right now and evaluate your own study environment:

1. Do you have one or two special places reserved just for studying? Or do you study wherever seems convenient or available at the time?

2. Is your study area a pleasant place? Would you offer it to a friend as a good place to study? Or do you dread it because it's so depressing?

3. How's the lighting? Is it too dim or too bright? Is the whole desk well-lit? Or only portions of it?

4. Are all the materials you need handy?

5. What else do you do here? Eat? Sleep? Write letters? Read for pleasure? If you try to study at the same place you sit to listen to your music or chat on the phone, you may find yourself doing one when you think you're doing the other!

6. Is your study area in a high-traffic or low-traffic area? How often are you interrupted by people passing through?

7. Can you close the door to the room to avoid disturbances and outside noise?

8. When do you spend the most time here? What time of day do you study? Is it when you are at your best, or do you inevitably study when you're tired and less productive?

9. Are your files, folders, and other class materials organized and near the work area? Do you have some filing system in place for them?

10. Set up a "future" drawer in your filing cabinet. When you find ideas, research material, and so forth (from magazines, books, newspapers, Web sites, wherever) that you think may be important *sometime in the future*, write a pertinent note to yourself and file it. The time you take now will be a mere fraction of the time you save in the future.

11. If you can afford it, take advantage of technology's efficiencies. For example, you can now buy a combination printer, fax, scanner, and copier for less than $500. Doesn't that beat paying a typist and donating quarters to the photocopier at the library?

Staying focused on your studies

If you find yourself doodling and dawdling more than reading and remembering, try these solutions:

Create a work environment in which you're comfortable. The size, style, and placement of your desk, chair, and lighting may all affect whether or not you're distracted from the work at hand. Take the time to design the area that's perfect for you. Needless to say, anything that you know will distract you — a girlfriend's picture, a radio or TV, whatever, should disappear from your study area.

Turn up the lights. Experiment with the placement and intensity of lighting in your study area until you find what works for you, both in terms of comfort and as a means of staying awake and focused.

Set some rules. Let family, relatives, and especially friends know how important your studying is and that specific hours are inviolate.

Take the breaks you need. Don't just follow well-intentioned but bogus advice about how long you should study before taking a break. Break when _you_ need to.

Fighting tiredness and boredom

You've chosen the best study spot and no one could fault you on its setup, but you're still using pencils to prop up your eyelids? Help is on the way:

Take a nap. What a concept! When you're too tired to study, take a short nap to revive yourself. Maximize that nap's effect by keeping it short — 20 minutes is ideal, 40 minutes absolute maximum. After that, you go into another phase of sleep and you may wake even more tired than before. If you can't take such short naps, train yourself to do so. I did during college out of necessity; my ability to nap virtually anywhere, anytime, and automatically wake after 20 minutes is one of my more useful talents.

Have a drink. A little caffeine won't harm you—a cup of coffee or tea, a glass of soda. Just be careful not to main-line it—caffeine's "wake-up" properties seem to reverse when you reach a certain level, making you far more tired than you were!

Turn down the heat. You needn't build an igloo out back, but too warm a room will inevitably leave you dreaming of sugarplums...while your paper remains unwritten on your desk.

Shake a leg. Go for a walk, high step around the kitchen, do a few jumping jacks—even mild physical exertion will give you an immediate lift.

Change your study schedule. Presuming you have some choice here, find a way to study when *you* are normally more awake and/or most efficient.

Studying with small kids

So many of you are going to school while raising a fam-ily, I want to give you some ideas that will help you cope with the Charge of the Preschool Light Brigade:

Plan activities to keep the kids occupied. The busier you are in school and/or at work, the more time your kids will want to spend with you when you *are* home. If you spend some time with them, it may be easier for them to play alone, especially if you've created projects *they* can work on while *you*'re working on your homework.

Make the kids part of your study routine. Kids love rou-tine, so why not include them in yours? If 4 p.m. to 6 p.m. is always "Mommy's Study Time," they will soon get used to it, especially if you make spending other time with them a prior-ity and if you take the time to give them something to do dur-ing those hours. Explaining the importance of what you're doing — in a way that includes some ultimate benefit for *them* — will also motivate them to be part of your "study team."

Use the television as a babysitter. While many of you will have a problem with this — it's one that I and my 11-year-old deal with weekly, if not daily — it may be the lesser of two evils. And you can certainly rent (or tape) enough quality shows so you don't have to worry about the little darlings watching street gangs bash skulls in (or bashing skulls themselves on some video game system).

Plan your study accordingly. Unless you are right up there in the Perfect Parent Pantheon, all these things will not keep your kids from interrupting every now and then. While you can minimize such intrusions, it's virtually impossible to eliminate them entirely. So don't try — plan your schedule *assuming* them. For one, that means taking more frequent breaks to spend five minutes with your kids. They'll be more likely to give you the 15 or 20 minutes at a time *you* need if they get periodic attention themselves. By default, *that* means avoiding projects that can only be done with an hour of massive concentration — you can only work in 15- or 20-minute bursts!

Find help. Spouses can occasionally take the kids out for dinner and a movie (and trust me, the kids will encourage you to study *more* if you institute this!), relatives can babysit (at their homes) on a rotating basis, playmates can be invited over (allowing you to send your darling to their house the next day), you may be able to trade babysitting chores with other parents at school, and professional daycare may be available at your child's school or in someone's home for a couple of hours a day.

Find out where *you* shine

It is the rare individual who is superior, or even good, in *every* subject. If you are, count your blessings. Most of us are a little better in one subject or another. Some of us simply *like* one subject more than another—and don't think *that* doesn't change your attitude toward it. Others are naturally gifted in one area, average in others.

For example, skill with numbers and spatial relations may come easily to you, but you may have absolutely no ear for music or languages. Or you may find learning a language to be a piece of cake, but not have the faintest clue why Pythagoras came up with his theorem—or why you should care. Some students are good with their hands. Others (I'm in this group) may find making the simplest item akin to torture.

The reasons for such unequal distribution of native-born talents rest somewhere in the area between karma and God, depending on your philosophy.

My advice is to be thankful for whatever native-born talents you possess and use the gift as a two-edged sword. Shift some study time from those tasks easily achieved to those that you find more difficult. The balance you will see in your development will be well worth the effort.

And if you've never really thought about the subjects you like and dislike, use the chart on page 62 to identify them. You'll also be asked to identify those in which you perform well or poorly. (Your report card should confirm those!) Use this list to organize your own schedule to take advantage of your natural talents and give added time to the subject areas that need the most work.

And if you have a choice

All college students—and some high school students—are able to pick and choose courses according to their own schedules, likes, dislikes, and goals, and so on. (There are exceptions, of course.) The headiness of such freedom should be tempered with the common-sense approach you're trying to develop through reading this book. Here are a few hints to help you along:

1. Whenever possible, consider each professor's reputation as you decide whether to select a particular course (especially if it is an overview or introductory course that is offered in two or three sections). Word soon gets around as to which professors' lectures are stimulating and rewarding—an environment in which learning is a joy, even if it isn't a subject you like!

2. Attempt to select classes so your schedule is balanced on a weekly, and even daily, basis, though this will not always be possible or advisable. (Don't change your major just to suit your schedule!) Try to leave an open hour or half-hour between classes—it's ideal for review, post-class note-taking, quick trips to the library, and so on.

3. Try to alternate challenging classes with those that come more easily to you. Studying is a process of positive reinforcement. You'll need encouragement along the way.

4. Avoid late-evening or early-morning classes, especially if such scheduling provides you with large gaps of "down time."

5. Set a personal study pace and follow it. Place yourself on a study diet, the key rule of which is: *Don't overeat.*

The landscape is littered with the shadows of unsuccessful students who have failed in their pursuits—*not* because they lacked the talent or motivation, but because they just overloaded on information and pressure.

You *can* be successful without killing yourself!

Evaluation of Subject Areas

List the subject areas/courses you like most:

_____

_____

_____

_____

_____

List those you like least:

_____

_____

_____

_____

_____

List the courses in which you get the best grades:

_____

_____

_____

_____

_____

And those in which you get the worst grades:

_____

_____

_____

_____

CHAPTER 3

How to Read and Remember

R EADING TRANSFORMS AND transports us through times past, present, and future. Nothing you will do as you pursue your studies will be as valuable as the reading skills you develop—they are your ultimate long-term learning tool. Presuming you agree, what do you do?

Define your purpose for reading

What is your purpose in reading? If the best answer you can come up with is, "Because my teacher said so," we need some better reasons. According to reading experts, there are six fundamental purposes for reading:

1. To grasp a certain message.
2. To find important details.
3. To answer a specific question.
4. To evaluate what you are reading.
5. To apply what you are reading.
6. To be entertained.

Use the clues in your textbooks

There are special sections found in nearly all textbooks and technical materials (in fact, in almost all books except novels) that contain a wealth of information and can help you glean more from your reading. Becoming familiar with this data will enrich your reading experience and often make it easier. Here's what to look for:

The first page after the title page is usually the *table of contents*—a chapter-by-chapter list of the book's contents. Some are surprisingly detailed, listing every major point or topic covered in each chapter.

The first prose section is the *preface* (after the title page, table of contents, and, perhaps, acknowledgments page, in which the author thanks other authors and his or her editor, typist, researcher, friends, relatives, teachers, and so forth—most of which can be ignored by the reader). It is usually a description of what information you will find in the book. Authors may also use the preface to point out unique aspects of their books.

The *introduction* may be in place of or in addition to the preface, written by the author or some "name" the author has recruited to lend additional prestige to his or her work. Most introductions are an even more detailed overview of the book—chapter-by-chapter summaries are often included to give the reader a feel for the material to be covered.

Footnotes may be found throughout the text (a slightly elevated number following a sentence or quote, e.g., "jim dandy"[24]) and either explained at the bottom of the page on which they appear or in a special section at the back of the text. Footnotes may be used to cite sources of direct quotes or ideas and/or to further explain a point, or to add information outside of the text. You may make it a habit to ferret out sources cited in this way for further reading.

If a text tends to use an alarmingly high number of terms with which you may not be familiar, the considerate author will include a _glossary_—essentially an abridged dictionary that defines all such terms.

The _bibliography_, usually at the end of the book, may include the source material the author used to research the textbook, a list of "recommended reading," or both. It is usually organized alphabetically by subject, making it easy for you to go to your library and find more information on a specific topic.

Appendices containing supplementary data or examples relating to subject matter covered in the text may also appear in the back of the book.

The last thing in a book is usually the _index_, an alphabetical listing that references, by page number, every mention of a particular name, subject, and topic in the text.

Making it a habit to utilize all of these tools in your textbooks can only make your studying easier.

Find other textbooks if necessary

While the authors and editors of most textbooks might well be experts, even legends, in a particular subject, writing in jargon-free, easy-to-grasp prose is probably not their strong suit. You will occasionally be assigned a textbook that is so obtuse you aren't even sure whether to read it front to back, upside down, or inside out.

If you find a particular chapter, section, or entire textbook as tough to read as getting your baby brother to do you a favor, get to the library or the bookstore and find *another* book covering the *same* subject area that you *can* understand.

If you just don't get it, maybe it's because the *author* just doesn't know how to *explain* it. *Maybe it's not your fault!* Too many students have sweated, moaned, dropped classes, even changed majors because they thought they were dumb, when it's possible it's the darned textbook that's dense, not you.

Use the clues in each chapter

Begin with a very quick overview of the assignment, looking for questions that you'd like answered. Consider the following elements of your reading assignment *before* you begin your reading.

Chapter titles and bold-faced subheads announce the detail about the main topic. And, in some textbooks, paragraph headings or bold-faced "lead-ins" announce that the author is about to provide finer details.

So start each reading assignment by going through the chapter, beginning to end, *reading* only *the bold-faced heads and subheads.*

Look for end-of-chapter summaries. Knowing what the author is driving at in a textbook will help you look for the important building blocks for his conclusions while you're reading.

Most textbooks, particularly those in the sciences, will have charts, graphs, numerical tables, maps, and other illustrations. Be sure to observe how they supplement the text and what points they emphasize, and make note of these.

In some textbooks, you'll discover that key terms and information are highlighted within the body text. To find the definitions of these terms may then be your purpose for reading.

Some textbook publishers use a format in which key points are emphasized by questions, either within the body of or at the end of the chapter. If you read these questions *before* reading the chapter, you'll have a better idea of what material you need to pay closer attention to.

If you begin your reading assignment by seeking out these heads, subheads, and other purpose-finding elements of the chapter, you'll have completed your prereading step. I advise that you *always* preread every assignment.

Three ways to read

Depending on what you're trying to accomplish in a particular reading assignment and the kind of book involved, there are three different ways to read. Knowing when to use each will make any assignment easier:

1. **Quick reference reading** focuses on seeking specific information that addresses a particular question/concern you might have.
2. **Critical reading** is used to discern ideas and concepts that require a thorough analysis.
3. **Aesthetic or pleasure reading** is for sheer entertainment or to appreciate an author's style and ability.

Skim first

The best way to begin any reading assignment is to skim the pages to get an overall view of what information is included. Then read the text carefully, word-for-word, and highlight the text and/or take notes in your notebook. (A brief digression: Most everyone I know confuses "skim" and "scan." Let me set the record straight. *Skim is to read quickly and superficially. Scan is to read carefully but for a specific item.* So when you skim a reading selection, you are reading it in its entirety, though you're only hitting the "highlights." When you scan a selection, you are reading it in detail but only until you find what you're looking for. Scanning is the *fastest* reading rate of all — although you are reading in detail, you are *not* seeking to comprehend or remember anything that you see until you find the bit of information you're looking for. I now trust none of you will ever confuse these words again!)

Newspapers make reading simple — gleaning the key news stories is as easy as reading the headlines and the first two or three paragraphs of each article.

Your textbooks are not always written to facilitate such an approach, but most of the authors probably make their key point of any paragraph in the first sentence of that paragraph. Succeeding sentences add details. In addition, most of your textbooks include helpful "callouts" — those brief notes or headings in the outside margins of each page that summarize the topic covered in the paragraph or section. Other books, such as this one, include headings and subheadings to organize the material.

These standard organizational tools should make your reading job simpler. The next time you have to read a history, geography, or similar text, try skimming the assigned pages first. Read the heads, the subheads, and the callouts. Read the first sentence of each paragraph. Then go back and start reading the details.

By beginning your reading with a 20-minute skim of the text, you should be ready to answer three questions:

1. What is the text's principal message or viewpoint?
2. Is an obvious chain of thought or reasoning revealed?
3. What major points are addressed?

While the heads, subheads, first sentences, and other author-provided hints we've talked about will help you get a quick read on what a chapter's about, some of the *words* in that chapter will help you concentrate on the important points and ignore the unimportant. Knowing when to speed up, slow down, ignore, or really concentrate will help you read both faster *and* more effectively.

When you see words and phrases such as "likewise," "in addition," "moreover," "furthermore," you should know nothing new is being introduced. If you already know what's going on, speed up or skip what's coming entirely.

On the other hand, when you see words and phrases such as "on the other hand," "nevertheless," "however," "rather," "but," and their ilk, slow down—you're getting information that adds a new perspective or contradicts what you've just read.

Lastly, watch out for "payoff" words such as, "in conclusion," "therefore," "thus," "consequently," and "to summarize," especially if you only have time to "hit the high points" of a chapter or if you're reviewing for a test. Here's where the real meat is. Slow down and pay attention!

Now go back for detail

If a more thorough reading is then required, turn back to the beginning. *Read one section (chapter, unit, whatever) at a time.*

As you read, make sure you know what's going on by asking yourself if the passage is written to address one of these questions:

1. **Who?** The paragraph focuses on a particular person or group of people. The topic sentence tells you *who* this is.

2. **When?** The paragraph is primarily concerned with *time.* The topic sentence may even begin with the word "when."

3. **Where?** The paragraph is oriented around a particular place or location. The topic sentence states *where* you are reading about.

4. **Why?** A paragraph that states reasons for some belief or happening usually addresses this question. The topic sentence answers *why* something is true or *why* an event happened.

5. **How?** A paragraph that identifies the way something works or the means by which something is done. The topic sentence explains the *how* of what is described.

Do not go on to the next chapter or section until you've completed the following exercise:

1. Write definitions of any key terms you feel are essential to understanding the topic.

2. Write questions and answers you feel clarify the topic.

3. Write any questions for which you *don't* have answers — then make sure you find them through rereading, further research, or asking another student or your teacher.

4. Even if you still have unanswered questions, move on to the next section and complete numbers one to three for that section. (And so on, until your reading assignment is complete.)

The challenge of technical texts

You've already learned a lot of ways to improve your reading. It's time to examine the unique challenges posed by highly technical texts — physics, trigonometry, chemistry, calculus — you know, subjects that three-fourths of all students avoid like the plague. More than any other kind of reading, these subjects demand a logical, organized approach, a step-by-step reading method. And they require a detection of the text's _organizational devices._

Developing the skill to identify the basic sequence of the text will enable you to follow the progression of thought, a progression that is vital to your comprehension and retention.

In most technical writing, each concept is a like a building block of understanding — if you don't understand a particular section or concept, you won't be able to understand the _next_ section, either.

Most technical books are saturated with ideas, terms, formulas, and theories. The chapters are dense with information, compressing a great wealth of ideas into a small space. They demand to be read very carefully.

In order to get as much as possible from such reading assignments, you can take advantage of some devices to make sense of the organization. Here are five basics to watch for:

1. Definitions and terms.
2. Examples.
3. Classifications and listings.
4. Use of contrast.
5. Cause-effect relationships.

In reading any specialized text, you must begin at the beginning — understanding the terms particular to that discipline. Familiar, everyday words have very precise definitions in technical writing. Everyday words can have a variety of meanings, some of them even contradictory, depending on the context in which they're used.

In contrast, in the sciences, terminology has fixed and specific meanings. For example, the definition of elasticity _(the ability of a solid to regain its shape after a deforming force has been applied)_ is the same in Las Vegas, London, or Lisbon.

Another communication tool is the example. Technical writing often is filled with new or foreign ideas—many of which are not readily digestible. They are difficult in part because they are abstract. Examples work to clarify these concepts, hopefully in terms more easily understood.

A third tool frequently utilized in texts is classification and listings. Classifying is the process by which common subjects are categorized under a general heading. Especially in technical writing, authors use classification to categorize extensive lists of detail. Such writings may have several categories and subcategories that organize these details into some manageable fashion.

A fourth tool used in communicating difficult information is that of comparing and contrasting. Texts use this tool to bring complicated material into focus by offering a similar or opposing picture. Through comparison, a text relates a concept to one that has been previously defined—or to one a reader may readily understand. Through contrast, the text concentrates on the differences and distinctions between two ideas. By focusing on distinguishing features, these ideas become clearer as one idea is held up against another.

A final tool that texts employ to communicate is the cause-effect relationship. This device is best defined in the context of science, where it is the fundamental quest of most scientific research. Science begins with the observation of the effect—what is happening? It is snowing. The next step is to conduct research into the cause: *Why* is it snowing? Detailing this cause-effect relationship is often the essence of scientific and technical writing.

Read with a plan

More than any other type of writing, highly specialized, technical writing must be read with a plan.

Your plan should incorporate the following guidelines:

1. **Learn the terms** that are essential to understanding the concepts presented.

2. **Determine the structure of the text.** Most chapters have a pattern that forms the skeleton for the material. Often it can be discerned through the contents page or titles and subtitles.

3. **Skim the chapter** to get a sense of the author's viewpoint. Ask questions to define your purpose in reading. Use any summaries or review questions to guide your reading.

4. **Do a thorough analytical reading** of the text. Do not proceed from one section to the next until you have a clear understanding of the section you are reading—the concepts generally build upon each other.

5. **Review immediately upon concluding your thorough reading.** Write a summary of the concepts and theories you need to remember. Answer any questions raised when you skimmed the text. Do the problems. If possible, apply the formulas.

Whether math and science come easily to you or make you want to find the nearest pencil-pocketed computer nerd and throttle him, there are some ways you can do better at such technical subjects:

✎ Whenever you can, "translate" formulas and numbers into words. To test your understanding, try to put your translation into _different_ words.

✎ Try translating a particularly vexing math problem into a drawing or diagram.

✎ Before you even get down to solving a problem, try to estimate the answer.

- ✎ Play around. There are often different paths to the same solution, or even equally valid solutions. If you find one, try to find others.

- ✎ When you are checking your calculations, try working *back*wards.

- ✎ Try to figure out what is being asked, what principles are involved, what information is important, and what's not.

- ✎ Teach someone else. Trying to explain mathematical concepts to someone will quickly pinpoint what you really know or don't know.

Reading foreign language texts

Foreign language texts should be approached the same way, especially basic ones teaching vocabulary. If you haven't mastered the words you're supposed to in the first section, you'll have trouble reading the story at the end of section three, even if you've learned all the words in sections two and three. So take it one step at a time and make sure you have mastered one concept, vocabulary list, lesson, and so forth, before jumping ahead.

Aesthetic (pleasure) reading

 To read a writer is for me not merely to get an idea of what he says, but to go off with him, and travel in his company.

— Andre Gide

Most fiction is an attempt to tell a story. There is a beginning, in which characters and setting are introduced.

There is a conflict or struggle that advances the story to a climax — where the conflict is resolved. A final _denouement_ or "winding up" unravels the conclusion of the story. Your literature class will address these parts using terms that are often more confusing than helpful. The following are brief definitions of some of the more important ones:

Plot. The order or sequence of the story — how it proceeds from opening through climax. Your ability to understand and appreciate literature depends upon how well you follow the plot — the _story_.

Characterization. The personalities or characters central to the story — the heroes, the heroines, the villains, and the supporting characters. You will want to identify the main characters of the story and their relationship to the struggle or conflict.

Theme. The controlling message or subject of the story, the moral or idea that the author is using the plot and characters to communicate.

Setting. The time and place in which the story occurs. This is especially important when reading a historical novel or one that takes you to another culture.

Point of view. Who is telling the story? Is it one of the central characters giving you flashbacks or a first-person perspective? Or is it a third-person narrator offering commentary and observations on the characters, the setting, and the plot?

The first step in reading literature is to familiarize yourself with these concepts, then try to recognize them in the novel or short story. As you begin your reading, approach it first from an aesthetic standpoint: How does it make you feel? What do you think of the characters? Do you like them? Hate them? Relate to them?

Second, make sure you know what's going on — this involves the plot and the development of the characters. On a chapter-by-chapter basis, you may find it helpful to keep a sheet of paper on which you can write a sentence or two of the plot development and note any new characters that are introduced.

How fast can you understand?

 When we read too fast or too slowly, we understand nothing.

—Pascal

Are you worried that you read too slowly? You probably shouldn't be — less-rapid readers are not necessarily less able. What counts is what you comprehend and remember. And like anything else, practice will probably increase your speed levels. If you must have a ranking, read the 300-word selection below from start to finish, noting the elapsed time on your watch. Score yourself as follows:

Less than 30 seconds	very fast
31-45 seconds	fast
46-60 seconds	high average
61-89 seconds	average
90-119 seconds	slow
120 seconds or more	very slow

Abdollah Nouri does not look like a dangerous counter-revolutionary. In a nation run by clerics, he ranks among the most senior, not quite an ayatullah but a *hojatolislam*, or "proof of Islam." His outspokenness is one reason the powers that be in Iran wish to destroy him.

This week Nouri will be called before a court to answer a 44-page indictment. He stands accused of dishonoring the Ayatullah Khomeini, undermining the authority of Iran's ruling clergy, and promoting relations with the U.S. If he is convicted, he faces a hefty fine, lashes of the whip, or a dozen years in prison. Much more critically, Nouri will then be disqualified from heading the reform ticket in next February's elections, thus ending any chance of his becoming the powerful speaker of Iran's 270-seat parliament, the Majlis-e-Shura. A victory by Nouri is crucial to his chief ally, the embattled reformist President of Iran, Mohammed Khatami, and his efforts to promote moderation, expand freedom, and normalize Iran's relations with the outside world.

This is not Nouri's first scuffle with hard-liners: In an impeachment trial last year, parliament ousted him as Minister of the Interior for permitting student demonstrations. Since then, his main vehicle of dissent has been the national daily *Khordad*. The newspaper has published antiregime opinions by prominent clerics, notably Grand Ayatullah Hossein Ali Montazeri, who has been under house arrest since 1997 for questioning *velayat-e-faqih*, the absolute authority of the clergy.

Being the patron and publisher of such notions has made Nouri one of the most popular politicians in Iran. [Khatami's] strategy is to send a flood of loyalist candidates to the election board, so that even if political stars like Nouri are barred, a solid number will survive the vetting process and get elected. Nouri praises Khatami for making government more accountable but warns that the President's program will face "serious problems" if reform forces are unfairly excluded from the next parliament.

Now answer the following questions *without referring back to the text:*

1. Nouri's chief ally is ___.
   a. the Ayatullah Khomeini
   b. the parliament
   c. Iran's president
   d. the *Khordad*

2. Nouri's main vehicle of dissent since his impeachment trial has been ___.
   a. the Ayatullah Khomeini
   b. the Majlis-e-Shura, Iran's parliament
   c. Mohammed Khatami, Iran's president
   d. the *Khordad*, the national daily newspaper

3. Which of the following has Nouri not been indicted for?
   a. undermining the authority of Iran's ruling clergy
   b. conspiring a government takeover
   c. promoting relations with the United States
   d. dishonoring the Ayatullah Khomeini

4. Iran's 270-seat parliament is called the ___.
   a. *Khordad*
   b. Ayatullah Khomeini
   c. Majlis-e-Shura
   d. *hojatolislam*

A good reader should be reading fast or very fast and have gotten at least three of the four questions correct. (Answers are at the end of the chapter.)

What decreases reading speed/comprehension

1. Reading aloud or moving your lips when you read.

2. Reading mechanically—using your finger to follow words and moving your head along as you read.
3. Applying the wrong *kind* of reading to the material.
4. Lacking a sufficient vocabulary.

There are several things you can do to improve these reading mechanics.

To increase your reading speed:

1. Focus your attention and concentration.
2. Eliminate outside distractions.
3. Provide for an uncluttered and comfortable environment.
4. Don't get hung up on single words or sentences, but *do* look up (in the dictionary) key words that you must understand in order to grasp an entire concept.
5. Try to grasp overall concepts rather than attempting to understand every detail.
6. If you find yourself moving your lips when you read (vocalization), practice reading with a pen or some other (nontoxic) object in your mouth. If it falls out while you're reading, you know you have to keep working!

To increase comprehension:

1. Try to make the act of learning sequential— comprehension is built by adding new knowledge to existing knowledge.
2. Review and rethink at designated points in your reading. Test yourself to see if the importance of the material is getting through.

3. If things don't add up, discard your conclusions. Go back, reread, and try to find an alternate conclusion.

4. Summarize what you've read, rephrasing it in your notes, in your own words.

Most importantly, read at the speed that's comfortable for you. Though I *can* read extremely fast, I *choose* to read novels much more slowly so I can appreciate the author's word play. Likewise, any material that I find particularly difficult to grasp slows me right down.

Should you take some sort of speed reading course, especially if your current speed level is slow? I can't see that it could particularly hurt you in any way. I can also, however, recommend that you simply keep practicing reading, which will increase your speed naturally.

Remembering what you read

In a world where the ability to master and remember a growing explosion of data is critical for individual success, too little attention is paid to the dynamics of memory and systems for improving it. Developing your memory is probably the most effective way to increase your efficiency, in reading and virtually everything else.

There are some basic tools that will help you remember what you read:

- ✎ **Understanding.** You will remember only what you understand. When you read something and grasp the message, you have begun the process of retention.

- ✎ **Desire.** You remember what you *choose* to remember. To remember the material, you must *want* to remember it and be convinced that you *will* remember it.

✎ **Overlearning.** To really remember what you learn, you should learn material thoroughly, or *over*learn. This involves prereading the text, doing a critical read, and having some definite means of review that reinforces what you should have learned.

✎ **Systematizing.** It's more difficult to remember random thoughts or numbers than those organized in some pattern. For example, which phone number is easier to remember: 538-6284 or 678-1234? Have a system to help you recall how information is organized and connected.

✎ **Association.** Mentally link new material to existing knowledge so that you are giving this new thought some context in your mind.

Retention

Retention is the process by which we keep imprints of past experiences in our minds, the "storage depot." Subject to other actions of the mind, what is retained can be recalled when needed. Things are retained in the same order in which they are learned. So your studying should build one fact, one idea, one concept upon another.

Broad concepts can be retained more easily than details. Master generalities and details will fall into place.

If you think something is important, you will retain it more easily. So convincing yourself that what you are studying is something you must retain (and recall) increases your chances of adding it to your storehouse.

Retention is primarily a product of what you understand. It has little to do with how *fast* you read, how great an outline you can construct, or how many fluorescent colors you can mark your textbooks with. Reading a text, grasping the message, and remembering it are the fundamentals that make for high-level retention. Reading at a 1,000-word-per-minute clip does not necessarily mean that you have a clue as to what a text really says.

As you work toward improving your reading, realize that speed is secondary to comprehension. If you can read an assignment faster than anyone in class, but can't give a one-sentence synopsis of what you just read, you lose. If you really get the author's message—even if it takes you an hour or two longer than some of your friends—your time will pay off in huge dividends in class and later in life.

Recall

This is the process by which we are able to bring forth those things that we have retained. Recall is subject to strengthening through the process of repetition. *Recall is least effective immediately after a first reading,* emphasizing the importance of review. The dynamics of our ability to recall are affected by several factors:

✎   We most easily recall those things that are of interest to us.

✎   Be selective in determining how much you need to recall. All information is not of equal importance—focus your attention on being able to recall the most *important* pieces of information.

✎   Allow yourself to react to what you're studying. Associating new information with what you already know will make it easier to recall.

✎   Repeat, either aloud or in your mind, what you want to remember. Find new ways of saying those things that you want to recall.

✎   Try to recall broad concepts instead of isolated facts.

✎   Use the new data you have managed to recall in a meaningful way — it will help you recall it the next time.

Recognition

This is the ability to see new material and recognize it for what it is and what it means. Familiarity is the key aspect of recognition — you will feel that you have "met" this information before, associate it with other data or circumstances, and then recall the framework in which it logically fits.

If you've ever envied a friend's seemingly wondrous ability to recall facts, dates, and telephone numbers virtually at will, take solace that, in most cases, _this skill is a result of study and practice_, not something he was born with.

There are certain fundamental memory systems that, when mastered, can significantly expand your capability. It is beyond the scope of this book to teach you these detailed techniques, but if you feel you need help, I recommend _Improve Your Memory_, another book in the _How to Study Program_. You'll probably find a number of helpful titles at your library as well.

Still having trouble?

If you followed the suggestions in this chapter and are still having trouble retaining what you read, try these other ideas.

Take notes

Do you own the book you're reading? Do you not care about preserving it for posterity? Then use its margins for notes. Go beyond mere highlighting to assign some ranking to the facts conveyed by the text.

I used to use a little shorthand method to help me remember written materials. I'd draw vertical lines close to the text to assign levels of importance. One vertical line meant that the material should be reviewed; two indicated that the facts were very important; asterisks would signify "learn or fail" material. I'd insert question marks for material that I wanted one of my more intelligent friends or the teacher to explain to me further. I'd use circles to indicate the information I was dead sure would show up on the next test.

Interestingly, I found that the very act of assigning relative weights of importance to the text and keeping a lookout for test material helped me remember because it heightened my attention.

Become an active reader

I urge you to quiz yourself on written material to ascertain how well you retain it. If this doesn't work, try asking the questions *before* you read the material.

For instance, even though I have been an avid reader throughout much of my academic life, I had some trouble with the reading comprehension sections of standardized tests the first couple of times I attempted them. Why? I think I had a tendency to rush through these sections.

Then someone suggested to me that I read the questions *before* I read the passage. Presto! Great scores in reading comprehension (765 points on my verbal SAT for all of you doubters!).

While you won't always have such a ready-made list of questions, there are other sources — the summaries at the beginnings of chapters, the synopses in tables of contents. Pay attention to these.

For instance, if an author states in an introductory paragraph, "Containing the Unsatisfactory Result of Oliver's

Adventure; and a Conversation of Some Importance between Harry Maylie and Rose," as Charles Dickens does in
Oliver Twist, you may ask yourself:

✎   What was Oliver's unsatisfactory adventure?

✎   What could the result of it have been?

✎   What could Harry and Rose be talking about
      that's so important?

Believe it or not, this technique will train your mind to
hone in on those important details when they arise in the
story. It would also be a good idea to ask yourself these questions immediately after you finish the chapter. It will help
you ascertain whether you "got" the important points of
the chapter and help you retain the information longer.

Understand, don't memorize

Approach any text with the intent of _understanding_ it
rather than memorizing it. Understanding is a key part of
memorization. Don't stop the flow of information during
your reading (other than to underline and take notes). Go
back and memorize later.

Organize the material

Our minds crave order. Optical illusions work because
the mind is bent on imposing order on every piece of information coming in from the senses. As you read, think of
ways to organize the material to help your mind absorb it.

I always liked diagrams with single words and short
phrases connected with arrows to show cause-and-effect relationships. Or I would highlight in texts the _reasons_ things
occurred with a special mark (I used a triangle).

Develop good reading habits

It's impossible for anyone to remember what he read at 3 a.m., or while waiting to go on the biggest date of his life. Set aside quiet time when you're at your best. Are you a morning person? Then wake up early to do your reading. Do you get going at 6 p.m.? Then get your reading done before stopping by the student union.

Don't forget to use your dictionary to look up terms you don't understand.

Why we forget

As you think about the elements of developing good memory, you can use them to address why you *forget*. The root of poor memory is usually found in one of these areas:

1. We fail to make the material meaningful.
2. We did not learn prerequisite material.
3. We fail to grasp what is to be remembered.
4. We do not have the desire to remember.
5. We allow apathy or boredom to dictate how we learn.
6. We have no set habit for learning.
7. We are disorganized and inefficient in our use of study time.
8. We do not use the knowledge we have gained.

In case you forgot

Each time you attempt to read something that you must recall, use this six-step process to assure you'll remember:

1. **Evaluate the material.** Define your purpose for reading. Identify your interest level and get a sense of how difficult the material is.

2. **Choose appropriate reading techniques** for the purpose of your reading. If you are reading to grasp the main idea, then that is exactly what you will recall.

3. **Identify the important facts** and remember what you need to. Let your purpose for reading dictate what you remember, and identify associations that connect the details to recall.

4. **Take notes.** Use your own words to give a synopsis of the main ideas. Use an outline, diagram, or concept tree to show relationship or pattern. Your notes serve as an important backup to your memory. Writing down key points will further reinforce your ability to remember.

5. **Review.** Quiz yourself on those things you *must* remember. Develop some system by which you review notes at least three times before you are required to recall. The first review should be shortly after you have read, the second should come a few days later, and the final review should take place just before you are expected to recall. This process will help you avoid cram sessions.

6. **Implement.** Find opportunities to *use* the knowledge you have gained. Study groups and class discussions are invaluable opportunities to put what you have learned to good use. Participate in group discussions — they'll greatly increase what you recall.

Build a library

 The reading of all good books is like conversation with the finest men of past centuries.

— Descartes

If you are ever to become an active, avid reader, access to books will do much to cultivate the habit. I suggest you "build" your own library. Your selections can and should reflect your own tastes and interests, but try to make them wide and varied. Include some of the classics, contemporary fiction, poetry, and biography.

Save your high school and college texts — you'll be amazed at how some of the material retains its relevance. And try to read a good newspaper every day to keep current and informed.

Your local librarian can refer you to any number of lists of the "great books," most of which are available in inexpensive paperback editions. Here are four more lists — compiled by yours truly — of the "great" classical authors; the "great" not-so-classical authors, poets, and playwrights; some contemporary "pretty greats"; and a selection of "great" works. You may want to put these on your buy list, especially if you're planning a summer reading program.

I'm sure that I have left off someone's favorite author or "important" title from these lists. They are not meant to be comprehensive, just representative. I doubt anyone would disagree that a person familiar with the majority of authors and works listed would be considered well-read!

Some "great" classical authors

Boccaccio	Aesop
Emerson	Aquinas

Cervantes	Homer
Chaucer	Horace
Aristotle	Nietzsche
J. Caesar	Plato
Balzac	Aeschylus
Cicero	Milton
Confucius	Montaigne
Kant	Plutarch
Dante	Flaubert
Descartes	Rousseau
Machiavelli	Voltaire
Goethe	Shakespeare
Dewey	Vergil
Erasmus	Ovid
Hegel	Santayana
Aristophanes	Swift
S. Johnson	Pindar
Spinoza	Burke

Some "great" not-so-classical authors

Sherwood Anderson	Albert Camus
W.H. Auden	Lewis Carroll
Samuel Beckett	Joseph Conrad
Brandan Behan	e.e. cummings
William Blake	Daniel Defoe
Bertolt Brecht	Charles Dickens
Charlotte Brontë	Emily Dickinson
Emily Brontë	Feodor Dostoevski
Pearl Buck	Arthur Conan Doyle
Lord Byron	Theodore Dreiser

Alexandre Dumas

George Eliot

T.S. Eliot

William Faulkner

Edna Ferber

F. Scott Fitzgerald

E.M. Forster

Robert Frost

John Galsworthy

Jose Ortega y Gasset

Nikolai Gogol

Maxim Gorki

Thomas Hardy

Nathaniel Hawthorne

Ernest Hemingway

Hermann Hesse

Victor Hugo

Aldous Huxley

Washington Irving

William James

James Joyce

Franz Kafka

John Keats

Rudyard Kipling

D.H. Lawrence

H.W. Longfellow

James Russell Lowell

Thomas Mann

W. Somerset Maugham

Herman Melville

H.L. Mencken

Henry Miller

H.H. Munro (Saki)

Vladimir Nabokov

O. Henry

Eugene O'Neill

George Orwell

Dorothy Parker

Edgar Allan Poe

Ezra Pound

Marcel Proust

Ellery Queen

Ayn Rand

Erich Maria Remarque

Bertrand Russell

J.D. Salinger

George Sand

Carl Sandburg

William Saroyan

Jean Paul Sartre

George Bernard Shaw

Percy Bysshe Shelley

Upton Sinclair

Aleksandr I. Solzhenitsyn

Gertrude Stein

Robert Louis Stevenson

Dylan Thomas

James Thurber

J.R.R. Tolkien

Leo Tolstoy

Ivan Turgenev
Mark Twain
Robert Penn Warren
Evelyn Waugh
H.G. Wells
Walt Whitman
Oscar Wilde

Thornton Wilder
Tennessee Williams
P.G. Wodehouse
Thomas Wolfe
William Wordsworth
William Butler Yeats
Emile Zola

Some "pretty great" contemporary authors

Edward Albee
Isaac Asimov
John Barth
Saul Bellow
T. Coraghessan Boyle
Anthony Burgess
Truman Capote
John Cheever
Don DeLillo
Pete Dexter
E. L. Doctorow
William Gaddis
William Golding
Robert Heinlein
Joseph Heller
Lillian Hellman
John Hersey
Oscar Hijuelos
Jerzy Kozinski

Norman Mailer
Bernard Malamud
Gabriel Garcia Marquez
Cormac McCarthy
Toni Morrison
Joyce Carol Oates
Flannery O'Connor
Thomas Pynchon
Philip Roth
Isaac Bashevis Singer
Jane Smiley
Wallace Stegner
Rex Stout
William Styron
Anne Tyler
John Updike
Alice Walker
Eudora Welty

Some "great" works

The Adventures of
  Huckleberry Finn

The Adventures of Tom Sawyer

The Aeneid

Aesop's Fables

Alice in Wonderland

All Quiet on the Western Front

An American Tragedy

Animal Farm

Anna Karenina

Arrowsmith

Atlas Shrugged

As I Lay Dying

Babbitt

The Bell Jar

Beloved

The Bonfire of the Vanities

Brave New World

The Brothers Karamazov

The Canterbury Tales

Catch-22

The Catcher in the Rye

Chimera

Confessions of an English
  Opium Eater

The Confessions of Nat Turner

The Count of Monte Cristo

Crime and Punishment

David Copperfield

Death Crimes for the
  Archbishop

Death of a Salesman

The Deerslayer

Demian

Don Juan

Don Quixote

Ethan Fromme

Far From
  the Maddening Crowd

A Farewell to Arms

The Federalist Papers

The Fixer

For Whom the Bell Tolls

The Foundation

A Good Scent From a Strange
Mountain

The Good Earth

The Grapes of Wrath

Gravity's Rainbow

The Great Gatsby

Gulliver's Travels

Hamlet

Heart of Darkness

The Hound of Baskervilles

I, Claudius

The Idiot

The Iliad

The Immortalist

The Invisible Man
Jane Eyre
JR
Julius Caesar
Kim
King Lear
Lady Chatterley's Lover
"Leaves of Grass"
The Legend of Sleepy Hollow
Les Miserables
A Lesson Before Dying
*A Long Day's Journey
   Into Night*
Look Homeward, Angel
Lord Jim
The Lord of the Rings
MacBeth
The Magic Mountain
Main Street
Man and Superman
The Merchant of Venice
The Metamorphosis
Moby Dick
Mother Courage
Native Son
1984
Of Human Bondage
Of Mice and Men
The Old Man and the Sea
Oliver Twist

*One Flew Over
   the Cuckoo's Nest*
The Optimist's Daughter
Othello
Our Town
Paradise Lost
The Pickwick Papers
The Picture of Dorian Gray
*A Portrait of the Artist
   as a Young Man*
Portrait of a Lady
Pride and Prejudice
The Prophet
Ragtime
"The Raven"
The Red Badge of Courage
*The Remembrance
   of Things Past*
The Return of the Native
"The Road Not Taken"
Robinson Crusoe
Romeo and Juliet
The Scarlet Letter
Siddhartha
Silas Marner
Sister Carrie
Sophie's Choice
The Sound and the Fury
Steppenwolf
A Streetcar Named Desire
The Sun Also Rises

The Tale of Genji	Ulysses
A Tale of Two Cities	Vanity Fair
Tender Is the Night	Walden
The Thin Red Line	War and Peace
The Time Machine	"The Wasteland"
A Thousand Acres	Winesburg, Ohio
Tom Jones	Wuthering Heights
The Trial	

Reading every one of these books will probably make you a better reader; it will certainly make you more well-read. That is the extra added bonus to establishing such a reading program—an appreciation of certain authors, certain books, certain cultural events, and the like is what separates the cultured from the merely educated and the undereducated.

Read on

Insofar as one can in a single chapter, I've tried to sum up the essentials of reading. It is not a finite science, but rather a skill and appreciation that one can develop over time. Good grade school training is essential. And for those of you who have been able to identify problem areas, there are always remedial classes.

If you feel you need more help with your reading comprehension, I urge you to consult *Improve Your Reading* and *Improve Your Memory*, both of which have also just been released in new editions.

CHAPTER 4

How to Organize Your Time

> Those who make the worst use of their time are the first to complain of its brevity.

—La Bruyere (1688)

WE ALL HAVE problems with time. We can't control it—we can't slow it down or speed it up. We can't save it up—all we can do is decide how we're going to spend it. We invariably need more of it, and don't know where to find it. *Then* we wonder where the heck it all went.

But *time* is not really the problem. After all, it's the one "currency" that all people are given in equal supply, every day. The problem is that most of us simply let too much of it slip through our fingers—because we have *never been taught how to manage our time*...or why we should try. Our parents never sat us down to give us a little "facts of time" talk, and time-management skills aren't part of any standard academic curriculum.

Whether you're a book author typing as fast as you can to meet a publisher's deadline, a student juggling five classes and a part-time job, or a parent working, attending classes, and raising a family, a simple, easy-to-follow time-management system is crucial to your success. And despite your natural inclination to proclaim that you just don't have the *time* to spend scheduling, listing, and recording, it's also the best way to give yourself *more* time.

There may *not* be enough time for everything

When I asked one busy student if she wished she had more time, she joked, "I'm *glad* there are only 24 hours in a day. Any more and I wouldn't have an excuse for not getting everything done!"

Let me give you the good news: There *is* a way that you can accomplish more in less time, one that's a *lot* more effective and doesn't even take more effort. You can plan ahead and make conscious choices about how your time will be spent, and how much time you will spend on each task. You can have more control over your time, rather than always running out of time as you keep trying to do everything.

Now the bad news: The first step to managing your time should be deciding just what is important…and what isn't. Difficult as it may be, sometimes it's necessary for us to recognize that we truly *can't* do it all—to slice from our busy schedules those activities that aren't as meaningful to us so that we can devote more energy to those that are.

But there *is* enough time to plan

Yet, even after paring down our commitments, most of us are still challenged to get it all done. What with classes, study time, work obligations, extracurricular activities, and a social life, it's not easy fitting it all in.

The time-management plan that I outline in this chapter is designed particularly for students. Whether you're in high school, college, or graduate school, a "traditional" student or one who's chosen to return to school after being out in the "real world" for awhile, you'll find that this is a manageable program that will work for you.

The purpose of this chapter is to help you make _choices_ about what is important to you, to help you set _goals_ for yourself, to help you _organize_ and _schedule_ your time, and to develop the _motivation_ and _self-discipline_ to follow your schedule and reach those goals, which will give you the time to learn all the other study skills I write about!

Identify the starting line

Like any of the skills I've already talked about in **How to Study**, you can't race off to your ultimate goal until you figure out where your starting line is. So the first step necessary to overhaul your current routine is to _identify_ that routine, in detail. My suggestion is to chart, in 15-minute increments, how you spend every minute of every day _right now_. While a day or two might be sufficient for some of you, I recommend you chart your activities for an entire week, including the weekend.

This is especially important if, like many people, you have huge pockets of time that seemingly disappear, but in reality are devoted to things like "resting" after you wake up, putting on makeup or shaving, reading the paper, waiting for transportation, or driving to and from school or work. Could you use an extra hour or two a day, either for studying or for fun? Make better use of such "dead" time and you'll find all the time you need.

For example, learn how to do multiple tasks at the same time. Listen to a book on tape while you're working around the house; practice vocabulary or math drills while you're driving; have your kids, parents, or roommates quiz you for an upcoming test while you're doing dishes, vacuuming, or dusting; and *always* carry your calendar, notebook(s), pens, and a textbook with you—you can get a phenomenal amount of reading or studying done while in line at the bank, in the library, at the supermarket, or on a bus or train.

Strategy tip: Identify those items on your daily calendar, whatever their priority, that can be completed in 15 minutes or less. These are the ideal tasks to tackle at the laundromat, while waiting for a librarian to locate a book you need, or while standing in line anywhere.

Collect what you need

As you begin your planning session, make sure you have all of the information and materials you need to make a quality plan. Gather your class syllabuses, work schedule, dates of important family events, vacations, trips, other personal commitments (doctor's appointments, parties), and a calendar of any extracurricular events in which you plan to participate.

Keeping track of your day-to-day activities (classes, appointments, regular daily homework assignments, and daily or weekly quizzes) will be dealt with after we talk about those projects (studying for midterms and finals, term papers, theses) that require completion over a long period—weeks, maybe even months.

Creating your Project Board

There are two excellent tools you can use for your long-term planning. The first is a Project Board, which you can put on any blank wall or right above your desk. You can buy a ready-made chart at an art or office supply store, stationery store, or bookstore. Or you can copy the format of the one I've included on pages 100 and 101.

How does the Project Board work? As you can see, it is just a variation on a calendar. I have set it up vertically — the months running down the left-hand side, the projects across the top. You can switch the order if you want. (Many store-bought charts come set up this way.)

Using your Project Board

In the case of each project, there is a key preparatory step before you can use the chart: You have to break down each general assignment into its component parts.

Next to each specific task, estimate the time you would expect to spend on it.

The more time you have to complete a project, the easier it is to procrastinate dealing with it, even to put off identifying the steps and working them into your regular schedule. If you find yourself leaving long-term projects to the last week, schedule the projects furthest away — the term paper due in three months, the oral exam 10 weeks from now — _first_. Then trick yourself — schedule the completion date at least seven days prior to the actual turn-in date, giving yourself a one-week cushion for life's inevitable surprises. (Just try to forget you've used this trick. Otherwise, you'll be like the perennial latecomer who set his watch 15 minutes fast in an effort to get somewhere on time — except he always reminded himself to add 15 minutes to the time on his wrist, defeating the whole purpose.)

For example, one project on the Sample Project Board involves working on a team with other students from your entrepreneurship class to create a hypothetical student business. While the steps are different from the other projects' components, you'll notice that the concept of breaking the

Sample Project Board

MONTH/WEEK	PROJECT: STUDENT CORPORATION
1st MONTH Week 1	Initial group meeting: Discuss overall assignment and possible products or services—bring list of three each to meeting (1 hour)
Week 2	Finalize product or service; finalize organization of group and long-term responsibilities of each subgroup (3)
Week 3	Subgroup planning and short-term assignments (2)
Week 4	Work on individual assignment from subgroup (2)
2nd MONTH Week 1	Work on individual assignment from subgroup (2)
Week 2	Work on individual assignment from subgroup (2)
Week 3	Integrate individual assignment with rest of subgroup (?)
Week 4	Meet with entire group to integrate plans (?)
3rd MONTH Week 1	Finalize all-group plan; draft initial report (?)
Week 2	Type and proof final report
Week 3	
Week 4	
DUE DATE	3RD MONTH/end of Week 2

PROJECT: DANTE TERM PAPER	REVIEW/EXAM SCHEDULE
Finalize topic (1 hour)	Review prior month's History notes (3)
Initial library research (2) General outline (1)	Review prior month's English notes (3)
Detailed library research (3)	Review prior month's Science notes (4)
Detailed library research (3)	Review prior month's Math notes (4)
Detailed library research (3)	Review 1st MONTH History notes (3)
Detailed outline (1)	Review 1st MONTH English notes (2)
First draft (4) Additional research (2)	Review 1st MONTH Science notes (4)
	Review 1st MONTH Math notes (4)
Second draft, spellcheck, proof (10)	2nd MONTH History notes (3)
Independent proof (1)	2nd MONTH English notes (2)
	2nd MONTH Science notes (4)
Type final draft and proof (4)	2nd MONTH Math notes (4)
end of 3RD MONTH	end of 3RD MONTH

project down into separate and manageable steps and allocating time for each doesn't change.

However, because time allocation in later steps depends on what assignments you're given by the group, we have had to temporarily place question marks next to some steps. As the details of this project become clearer and specific assignments are made, your Project Board should be changed to reflect both more details and the specific time required for each step.

You should also include on your Project Board time for studying for all of your final exams. You've decided that every Sunday morning is "review time" and allocated one Sunday a month to review the previous month's work in each subject.

Keep adding any other important projects throughout the term and continue to revise it according to actual time spent as opposed to time allocated. Getting into this habit will make you more aware of how much time to allocate to future projects and make sure that the more you do so, the more accurate your estimates will be.

Using a Term Planning Calendar

The Term Planning Calendar should be used in concert with the Project Board.

Start by transferring all the information from the Project Board to your Term Planning Calendar. Then add your weekly class schedule, work schedule, family celebrations, vacations and trips, club meetings, and extracurricular activities—everything. The idea is to make sure your Term Planning Calendar has *all* the scheduling information, while your Project Board contains just the briefest summary that you can ingest at a glance.

Leave your Project Board on your wall at home; carry your Term Planning Calendar with you. Whenever new projects, appointments, or meetings are scheduled, add them to your calendar immediately. Then transfer the steps involving major projects to your Project Board.

High school students may find it quite easy to use only the calendar, as they are usually not subject to quite as many long-term projects as college or graduate students. But once you're in college, especially if you have more than an average number of papers, reports, or projects, you'll find the Project Board a very helpful extra tool.

Planning your days and weeks

For any time-management system to work, it has to be used continually. Make an appointment with yourself at the end of each week—Sunday night is perfect—to sit down and plan for the following week. This may just be the best time you spend all week, because you will reap the benefits of it throughout the week and beyond.

Step 1: Make a "to-do" list

First, you must identify everything you need to do _this week_. Look at your Project Board and/or Term Planning Calendar to determine what tasks need to be completed this week for all your major school projects. Add any other tasks that must be done this week, from sending off a birthday present to your sister to attending your monthly volunteer meeting to completing homework that may have just been assigned.

Remember to break any long-term or difficult projects into small, "bite-size" tasks that can be included on your schedule. As Henry Ford said, "Nothing is particularly hard if you divide it into small jobs." Hence, the assembly line.

TERM PLANNING CALENDAR

Fill in due dates for assignments and papers, dates of tests, and important non-academic activities and events.

Month	MON	TUE	WED	THU	FRI	SAT	SUN

Step 2: Prioritize your tasks

When you sit down to study without a plan, you just dive into the first project that comes to mind. Of course, there's no guarantee that the first thing that comes to mind will be the most important. The point of the weekly Priority Task Sheet is to help you arrange your tasks _in order of importance._ That way, even if you find yourself without enough time for everything, you can at least finish those assignments that are most important. You can't effectively deal with _today's_ priorities if you still have to contend with yesterday's...or last week's! A completed sample is on page 107, and a blank form for you to photocopy and use is on page 115 of this book.

First, ask yourself this: If I only got a few things done this week, what would I want them to be? Mark these high-priority tasks with an "H." After you have identified the "urgent" items, consider those tasks that are _least_ important—items that could wait until the following week to be done, if necessary. You may have tasks that you consider very important, but don't have to be completed this week. These items might be less important this week, but are likely to be rated higher next week. These are low-priority items; mark them with an "L."

Strategy tip: If you push aside the same low-priority item day after day, week after week, at some point you should just stop and decide whether it's something you need to do at all! This is a strategic way to make a task or problem "disappear." In the business world, some managers purposefully avoid confronting a number of problems, waiting to see which will simply solve themselves through benign neglect. If it works in business, it can work for you in school.

All other responsibilities fit somewhere between the critical tasks and those of low priority. Review the remaining items, and if you are sure that none of them are either "H" or "L," mark them with an "M" (to represent middle priority).

Step 3: Fill in your Daily Schedule

Before you start adding papers, projects, homework, study time, and so forth, to your calendar, fill in the "givens" — the time you need to sleep, eat, work, and attend class. Even if your current routine consists of meals on the run and sleep wherever you find it, build the assumption *right into your schedule* that you are going to get eight hours of sleep and three decent meals a day. You may surprise yourself and find that there is still enough time to do everything you need. (Though all of us probably know someone who sleeps three hours a night, eats nothing but junk, and still finds a way to get straight A's, most experts would contend that regular, healthy eating and a decent sleep schedule are key attributes of any successful study system.)

Now transfer the items on your Priority Task Sheet to your Daily Schedule forms. (See page 108 for a sample completed schedule, and page 116 for a form you can photocopy.) Put in the "H" items first, followed by the "M" items. Then, fit in as many of the "L" items for which you still have room.

By following this procedure, you'll make sure you give the amount of time needed to your most important priorities. You can devote your most productive study times to your most important tasks, and plug in your lower priorities as they fit.

Besides the importance of the task and the available time you have to complete it, other factors will determine how you fit your Daily Schedules together. Some will be beyond your control: work schedules, appointments with professors, counselors, and doctors, and so on. But there are plenty of factors you *do* control, which you should consider as you put together your Daily Schedules for the week.

Don't overdo it. Plan your study time in blocks, breaking up work time with short leisure activities. It's helpful to

Priority Rating	Scheduled?	**PRIORITY TASKS THIS WEEK**
		Week of **3/28** through **4/3**
		Sociology Paper
H		* Library search
M		* Outline
L		* Rough draft
		Math assignments
H		* Chap. 4
M		* Chap. 5
M		* Study for test

DAILY SCHEDULE   Date: 3/30

Assignments Due	Schedule
Bio lab work	5
Math, chap. 4	6
	7
	8
	9 Biology
To Do/Errands	10 Sociology
Call John J.	11 ↓
Books to library	12 Lunch with Kim
Bank	1 Read Soc chap. 5
Groceries	2 ↓
Drop by Jim's	3 Math
	4 travel
	5
Homework	6 Math homework
Math Chap. 5 #1-9	7 work on paper
Sociology paper	8 ↓ ↓
(rough draft)	9
	10
	11
	12

add these to your schedule as well. You'll find that these breaks help you think more clearly and creatively when you get back to studying.

Even if you tend to like longer blocks of study time, be careful about scheduling study "marathons" — six- or eight-hour stretches rather than a series of two-hour sessions. The longer the period you schedule, the more likely you'll have to fight the demons of procrastination. Convincing yourself that you are really studying your heart out, you'll also find it easier to justify time-wasting distractions, scheduling longer breaks, and, before long, quitting before you should.

Make sure you use your Daily Schedule *daily*. That's what it's there for. Each night (or when you wake up in the morning) look at your schedule for the upcoming day. How much free time is there? Are there "surprise" tasks that are not on your schedule but need to be? Are there conflicts you were not aware of at the beginning of the week? By checking your Daily Schedule *daily*, you'll be able to respond to these changes.

Finally, remember Parkinson's Law: Work expands so as to fill the time available for its completion. In other words, if you fail to schedule a one-hour block for a project that *should* take an hour, you will probably be surprised to find that (eureka!) it somehow takes two or three.

Strategy tip: Get into the habit of getting ready for the next day before you go to bed the night before. Believe me, it's an absolutely fantastic feeling to *start* the day completely organized...especially if you oversleep!

Using these tools effectively

There are thinkers and there are doers.

Then there are those who think a lot about doing.

Organizing your life requires you to actually *use* the Project Board, Term Planning Calendar, Priority Task Sheets, and Daily Schedules. Once you have discovered habits and patterns of study that work for you, continue to use and hone them. Be flexible enough to add techniques you learn from others and alter schedules that circumstances have made obsolete.

Plan according to *your* schedule, *your* goals, and *your* aptitudes, not some ephemeral "standard." Allocate the time you expect a project to take *you*, not the time it might take someone else or how long your teacher says it should take. Try to be realistic and honest with yourself when determining those things that require more effort or those that come easier to you.

Whenever possible, schedule pleasurable activities *after* study time, not before. They will then act as incentives, not distractions.

Monitor your progress at reasonable periods and make changes where necessary. This is *your* study regimen—you conceived it, you can change it. If you find that you are consistently allotting more time than necessary to a specific chore, change your future schedule accordingly.

As assignments are entered on your calendar, make sure you also enter items needed—texts; other books you have to buy, borrow, or get from the library; and materials such as drawing pads, magic markers, and graph paper.

You may decide that color-coding your calendar—say, red for assignments that must be accomplished that week, blue for steps in longer-term assignments, yellow for personal time and appointments, green for classes—makes it easier for you to tell at a glance what you need to do and when you need to do it.

Adapt these tools for your own use. Try anything you think may work—use it if it does, discard it if it doesn't.

Do your least favorite chores (study assignments, projects, whatever) first—you'll feel better having gotten them out of the way! And plan how to accomplish them as meticulously as possible. That will get rid of them even faster.

Accomplish one task before going on to the next one — don't skip around.

If you see that you are moving along faster than you anticipated on one task or project sequence, there is absolutely nothing wrong with continuing onto the next part of that assignment or the next project step.

If you're behind, don't panic. Just reorganize your schedule and find the time you need to make up.

Write things down. Not having to remember all these items will free up space in your brain for the things you need to concentrate on or *do* have to remember.

Learn to manage distractions. As a time-management axiom puts it, "Don't respond to the urgent and forget the important." Some things you do can be picked up or dropped at any time. Beware of these time-consuming and complicated tasks that, once begun, demand to be completed. Interrupting at any point might mean starting all over again. What a waste of time *that* would be!

If you're writing and you have a brainstorm just as the phone rings (and you know it's from that person you've been waiting to hear from all week), take a minute to at least jot down your ideas before you stop.

Nothing can be as counterproductive as losing your concentration, especially at critical times. Learn to ward off those enemies that would alter your course and you will find your journey much smoother.

One way to guard against these mental intrusions is to know your own study clock and plan accordingly. Each of us is predisposed to function most efficiently at specific times of day (or night). Find out what sort of study clock you are on and schedule your work during this period.

Beware of uninvited guests and *all* phone calls: Unless you are ready for a break, they'll only get you off schedule. More subtle enemies include the sudden desire to sharpen every pencil in the house, an unheard-of urge to clean your room, an offer to do your sister's homework. Anything to avoid your own work. If you find yourself doing anything but your work, either take a break then and there, or pull yourself together and get down to work. Self-discipline, too, is a learned habit that gets easier with practice.

The simple act of saying no (to others or to yourself) will help insulate you from these unnecessary (and post-ponable) interruptions. Remember, what you are seeking to achieve is not just time—but *quality* time. Put your "Do not disturb" sign up and stick to your guns, no matter what the temptation.

Remember that time is relative. Car trips take longer if you have to schedule frequent stops for gas, food, and necessities, longer still if you start out during rush hour. Likewise, libraries are more crowded at certain times of the day or year, which will affect how fast you can get books you need, etc. So take the time of day into account.

And if your schedule involves working with others, you need to take *their* sense of time into account—you may find you have to schedule "waiting time" for a chronically late friend...and always bring a book along.

A special note for commuters

If you live at home (as opposed to being housed on campus), there are some special pressures with which you need to contend.

Your commute to school will probably be longer than if you could roll out of bed and walk to class. It will certainly require more wakefulness, even if you just have to stumble to a subway or bus (but especially if you have to drive!).

You'll also have travel time problems if you need to return to the campus for any reason after you've gone home. It's especially important that _you_ minimize travel time, planning enough to maximize your use of the campus facilities without scheduling a trip home in between.

While nobody likes walking to class in rain, sleet, or snow — except, perhaps, future postal employees — it is invariably easier to walk a few tree-lined blocks than drive a few miles in inclement weather. Take weather problems into account when scheduling your commute.

The very act of living at home — whether as a child or one "married with children" — brings with it responsibilities to others you could minimize living in a dorm. Be ready to allocate time to these responsibilities and include them in your study schedule. They're as inevitable if you live at home as meatloaf on Tuesdays.

Now comes the payoff

Once you start using your Project Board, Term Planning Calendar, Priority Task Sheets, and Daily Schedules, you will reap the benefits every day.

Anything — even school — seems less overwhelming when you have it broken into "bite-size" pieces...and you already know the flavor.

You no longer worry about when you'll get that paper done — you've already planned for it.

More time than ever before

My time-management program allows for flexibility. In fact, I encourage you to adapt any of my recommendations to your own unique needs. That means it will work for you whether you are living in a dorm, sharing an apartment or house with roommates, or living with a spouse and children. You *can* learn how to balance school, work, fun, and even family obligations.

As you get used to managing your time, planning well ahead as well as planning your week and even your days, you'll quickly discover that you seem to have more time than ever before.

Priority Rating	Scheduled?	**PRIORITY TASKS THIS WEEK**
		Week of ▨▨▨▨ through ▨▨▨▨

DAILY SCHEDULE   Date:

Assignments Due	Schedule
	5
	6
	7
	8
	9
To Do/Errands	10
	11
	12
	1
	2
	3
	4
	5
Homework	6
	7
	8
	9
	10
	11
	12

CHAPTER 5

How to Excel in Class

HATEVER YOUR GRADE level, whatever your grades, whatever your major, whatever your ultimate career goal, all of us have one thing in common: the classroom experience.

Most teachers utilize the classroom setting as an opportunity to embellish and interpret material covered in the text and other assigned readings. If you always complete your reading assignments before class, you'll be able to devote your classroom time to the "add-on" angles the teacher will undoubtedly cover.

You've got to have class

Exactly how you'll use the skills we'll cover in this chapter will be influenced by two factors: the type of classroom setup and the particular methods and styles employed by each of your teachers.

Each of the following general class formats will require you to make adjustments to accomplish your goals.

Lectures: Podium pleasantries

Teacher speaks, students listen. Pure lectures are quite common from the college level up, but exist only rarely at the high school level. Lecture halls at larger colleges may fill up with hundreds of students for some of the more popular courses (or introductory classes, particularly in the sciences).

Primary emphases: listening; note-taking.

Discussions: Time to speak your mind

Also called *tutorials* and *seminars*, discussion groups are again common on the college level, often as adjuncts to courses boasting particularly large enrollments. A typical weekly schedule for such a course might consist of two lectures and one or more discussion groups. Often led by graduate teaching assistants, these discussion groups contain fewer students — usually no more than two dozen — and give you the chance to discuss points made in the lecture and material from assigned readings.

Such groups rarely follow a precise text or format and may wander wildly from topic to topic, once again pointing out the need for a general mastery of the course material, the jumping-off point for discussion.

Primary emphases: asking/answering questions; analyzing concepts and ideas; taking part in discussion.

Combination: Best (or worst) of both

Some post-secondary courses are, for want of a better term, combination classes—they combine the lecture and discussion formats (pretty much the typical kind of pre-college class you're used to). The teacher prepares a lesson plan of material he or she wants to cover in a specific class. Through lecture, discussion, question and answer, audiovisual presentation, or a combination of one or more such devices, the material is covered.

Your preparation for this type of class will depend to a great extent on the approach of each individual instructor. Such classes also occur on the post-secondary level—college, graduate school, trade school—when class size is too small for a formal lecture approach.

Primary emphases: note-taking; listening; participation; asking and answering questions.

Getting your hands dirty

Classes such as science labs and various vocational education courses (industrial arts, graphics, and so forth) occur at all levels from high school up. They are concerned almost exclusively with _doing_ something—completing a particular experiment, working on a project, whatever. The teacher may demonstrate certain things before letting the students work on their own, but the primary emphasis is on the student carrying out his or her own projects while in class.

On the college level, science labs are merely overseen by graduate assistants. Trade schools may use a combination of short lectures, demonstrations, and hands-on workshops; you can't become a good auto mechanic just by reading a book on cleaning a distributor.

Primary emphasis: development and application of particular manual and technical skills.

Exceptions to the rule

Rarely can a single class be neatly pigeonholed into one of these formats, though virtually all will be primarily one or another. It would seem that size is a key factor in choosing a format, but you can't always assume, for example, that a large lecture course, filled with 200 or more students, will feature a professor standing behind a rostrum reading from his prepared text. Or that a small class of a dozen people will tend to be all discussion.

During my college years, I had a religion teacher who, though his class was one of the more popular on campus and regularly drew 300 or more students to each session, rarely lectured at all. I never knew *what* to expect when entering his classroom. One week it would be a series of musical improvisations from a local jazz band, with a variety of graduate assistants talking about out-of-body (religious, note the tie-in) experiences. Another session would consist entirely of the professor arguing with a single student over one key topic...which had *nothing* to do with that week's (or any *other* week's) assignment.

In another class of merely 20 students, the professor teaching us physical chemistry would march in at the sound of the bell and, without acknowledging anyone's presence or saying a word, walk to the blackboard and start writing equations, which he would continue to do, working his way across the massive board, until, some 20 or 30 minutes later, he ran off the right side. Slowly, he would walk back to the left side...and start writing all over again. He never asked questions. Never asked *for* questions. In fact, I'm not sure I remember him uttering *any*thing for three solid months!

Know your teacher

What is also extremely important for you to know and understand is the kind of teacher you've got, his likes, dislikes, preferences, style, and what he expects you to get out of his class. Depending on your analysis of your teacher's habits, goals, and tendencies, preparation may vary quite a bit, whatever the chosen format.

Some teachers are very confident fielding questions at any point during a lesson; others prefer questions to be held until the end of the lesson; still others (my chemistry prof is a good example) discourage questions (or any interaction for that matter) entirely. Learn when and how your teacher likes to answer questions and ask accordingly.

No matter how ready a class is to enter into a freewheeling discussion, some teachers fear losing control and veering away from their very specific lesson plan. Such teachers may well encourage discussion but always try to steer it into the set path they've decided upon. Other teachers thrive on chaos, in which case you can never be sure just what's going to happen.

Approaching a class with the former teacher should lead you to participate as much as possible in the class discussion, but warn you to stay within whatever boundaries he or she has obviously set.

Getting ready for a class taught by the latter kind of teacher requires much more than just reading the text—there will be a lot of emphasis on your understanding key concepts, interpretation, and analysis, as well as your ability to apply those lessons to cases or problems never mentioned in your text at all!

Some teachers' lesson plans or lectures are, at worst, a review of what's in the text and, at best, a review plus some discussion of sticky points or areas he or she feels may give you problems. Others use the text or other assignments merely as a jumping-off point—their lectures or lesson plans might cover numerous points that aren't in your text at all! Preparing for the latter kind of class will require much more than rote memorization of facts and figures—you'll have to be ready to give examples, explain concepts in context, and more.

Most of your teachers and professors will probably have the same goals: to teach you how to think, learn important facts and principles of the specific subject they teach, and, perhaps, how to apply them in your own way.

In math or science classes, your ability to apply what you've learned to specific problems is paramount.

Others, such as English, will require you to analyze and interpret various works, but may emphasize the "correct" interpretation, too.

Whatever situation you find yourself in — and you may well have one or more of each of the above "types" — you will need to adapt the skills we will cover in this chapter to each.

Adapt to your teacher's style

Building a note-taking strategy around each teacher's typical "plan of attack" for lectures is another key to academic success. Why do some students just seem to know what's important and what's not? How do they ferret out exactly the information that's "test-worthy" while not even glancing at the material that isn't?

What these students innately know is that items discussed during *any* lesson can be grouped into several categories:

✎   **Information** not contained in the class text(s) or other assigned reading.

✎   **Explanations** of obscure material covered in the text but with which students may have difficulty.

✎   **Demonstrations** or examples to further explain a concept, process, or subject.

✎ **Background information** to put course
material in context.

As you listen to your teacher, try to figure out which
category his remarks fall into. This will help you determine
the extent and detail of your notes on that segment of the
lecture.

How to prepare for any class

In general, here's how you should plan to prepare for
any class before you walk through the door and take your
seat.

Complete all assignments

Regardless of a particular teacher's style or the classroom
format he or she is using, virtually every course you take
will have a formal text (or two or three or more) assigned to
it. Though the way the text explains or covers particular topics may differ substantially from your teacher's approach to
the same material, your text is still the basis of the course
and a key ingredient in your studying. You _must_ read it,
plus any other assigned books, _before_ you get to class.

You may sometimes feel you can get away without
reading assigned books beforehand, especially in a lecture
format where you _know_ the chance of being called on is
somewhere between slim and none. But fear of being ques-
tioned on the material is certainly not the only reason I stress
reading what's been assigned. You will be lost if the professor decides—for the first time ever!—to spend the entire
period asking _the students_ questions. I've had it happen. And
it is _not_ a pleasant experience for the unprepared.

You'll also find it harder to take clear and concise notes
because you won't know what's in the text (in which case

you'll be frantically taking notes on material you could have underlined in your books the night before—if you had read them, of course) or be able to differentiate between important and useless information.

If you're heading for a discussion group, how can you participate without your reading as a basis? I think the lousiest feeling in the world is sitting in a classroom knowing that, sooner or later, you are going to be called on, and you don't know the material.

Remember: This includes not just reading the main text but any other books, articles, handouts, and so forth, previously assigned. It also means completing any nonreading assignments—turning in a lab report, preparing a list of topics, being ready to present your oral report.

Review your notes

Both from your reading and from the previous class. Your teacher is probably going to start this lecture or discussion from the point he or she left off last time. And you probably won't remember where that point was, unless you check your notes.

Have questions ready

As I discussed in Chapter 3, preparing questions as you read text material is an important step. This is your chance to find the answers to the questions that are still puzzling you. Review your questions before class. That way, you'll be able to check off the ones the lecturer or teacher answers along the way and you'll only need to ask those left unanswered.

Prepare your attitude

Don't discount the importance of the way you approach each class mentally. Getting the most out of school in general and any class in particular depends in good measure on how ready you are to really take part in the process. It is *not* sufficient, even if you're otherwise well-prepared, to just sit back and absorb the information. Learning requires your active participation every step of the way.

What to do in class

Keep in mind your own preferences and under what circumstances you do best—refer back to the first two chapters and review your skills lists. You'll need to concentrate hardest on those courses in which you do most poorly, no matter what the teacher's style.

Sit near the front

Reduce distraction as much as possible by sitting as close to the instructor as you can.

You've probably realized by now that the farther you sit from the teacher, the more difficult it is to listen. Sitting toward the back of the room means more heads bobbing around in front of you and more students staring out the window…and encouraging you to do the same.

Sitting up front has several benefits. You'll make a terrific impression on the instructor since you might be the only student in the front row. He'll see immediately that you have come to class to listen and learn, not just take up space. You'll be able to hear the instructor's voice clearly, and the instructor will be able to hear *you* clearly.

Finally, being able to see the teacher clearly will help ensure that your eyes don't wander around the room and out the window, taking your brain with them. If you have the option of picking your seat, head right for the head of the class(room).

Avoid distracting classmates

The gum-cracker. The doodler. The practical jokester. The whisperer. Even the perfume-sprayer. Your fellow classmates may be kind and thoughtful friends, entertaining lunch companions, and great fun at parties, but their little quirks, idiosyncrasies, and personal hygiene habits can prove distracting when you sit next to them in class. Knuckle-cracking and note-passing are just some of the evils that can divert your attention in the middle of your biology professor's discourse on bivalves. Avoid them.

Sit up straight

Do I sound like your mother? I know you don't want to hear it, but she's right. To listen effectively, you must sit in such a way that will let you stay comfortable and relatively still during the entire lecture. If parts of your body start to ache or fall asleep, your attention will inevitably wander. Remember: "The mind can retain only as much as the bottom can sustain."

Listen for verbal clues

Identifying noteworthy material means separating the wheat—that which you should write down—from the chaff—that which you should ignore. Do that by *listening* for verbal clues and *watching* for nonverbal ones.

Certainly not all teachers will give you the clues you're seeking. But many will invariably signal important material in the way they present it—pausing (waiting for all the pens to rise); repeating the same point (perhaps even one already made and repeated in your textbook); slowing down their normally supersonic lecture speed; speaking more loudly (or more softly); even stating, "I think the following is important."

There are also a number of words and phrases that should *signal* noteworthy material (and, at the same time, give you the clues you need to logically organize those notes at the same time): "First of all," "Most importantly," "Therefore," "As a result," "To summarize," "On the other hand," "On the contrary," "The following (number of) reasons (or causes, effects, decisions, facts, and so on)."

These (and similar words and phrases I'm sure you can think of) give you the clues to not just write down the material that follows, but to put it in context—to make a list ("First," "The following reasons"); establish a cause-and-effect relationship ("Therefore," "As a result"); establish opposites or alternatives ("On the other hand," "On the contrary"); signify a conclusion ("Therefore," "To summarize"); or offer an explanation or definition.

Watch for nonverbal clues

Studies have shown that only a fraction of communication is carried in words themselves. A great deal of the message we receive when someone is speaking to us comes from body language, facial expression, and tone of voice.

Most instructors will go off on tangents of varying relevance to the subject matter. Some of these will be important, but, at least during your first few lessons with that particular teacher, you won't know which.

Body language can be your clue. If the teacher begins looking at the window or his eyes glaze over, he's sending a clear signal: This won't be on any test.

On the other hand, if he turns to write something down on the blackboard, makes eye contact with several students, and/or gestures dramatically, he's sending a very obvious signal about the importance of the point he's making.

Of course, there are exceptions to this rule. There was a trigonometry professor I endured who would get most worked up about the damage being done to the nation's sidewalks by the deadly menace of chewing gum.

Teachers like to see students take notes. It shows you are interested in the topic and that you think enough of what is being said to write it down. (And, if you've ever stood at the front of the room, you can usually tell who's taking notes and who's writing a letter to a friend in Iowa.)

Ask questions

No, don't raise your hand to ask or answer questions every 90 seconds. Being an active listener means asking *yourself* if you understand everything that has been discussed. If the answer is no, ask the instructor questions at an appropriate time or write down questions that you must have answered to understand the subject fully.

Challenge yourself to draw conclusions from the things the instructor is saying. Don't just sit there letting your hand take notes. Let your mind do something, too. Think about the subject matter, how it relates to what you've been assigned to read and other facts to which you've been exposed.

To tape or not to tape

I am opposed to using a tape recorder as a substitute for an active brain in the classroom for quite a number of reasons:

- ✎ **It is time-consuming.** To be cynical about it, not only will you have to waste time sitting in class, you'll have to waste more time listening to that class *again*!

- ✎ **It is virtually useless for review.** Rewinding and fast forwarding through cassettes to find the salient points of a lecture is my definition of torture. During the hectic days before an exam, are you really going to want to waste time listening to a lecture when you can read so much more quickly?

 It offers no backup. Only the most diligent of students will tape record *and* take notes. So what happens if your tape recorder malfunctions? How useful will blank or distorted tapes be when it comes time for you to review? If you're going to take notes anyway, as a method of backup, why not just do a good job and save yourself the time and effort of listening to that lecture over again?

It costs money. Compare the price of blank paper and a pen to that of a recorder, batteries, and tapes. The cost of batteries *alone* should convince you that you're better off going the low-tech route.

You miss those "live" clues we discussed earlier. When all you have is a tape of your lecture, you don't see that zealous flash in your teacher's eyes, the passionate arm-flailing, the stern set of the jaw, all of which should scream, "Listen up! This will be on your test!"

I do concede, however, that there are situations in which tape recorders can be useful—such as when your head is so stuffed up with a cold that "active listening" during an hour-long lecture is virtually impossible. With this exception noted, I still maintain that a tape recorder is no substitute for good listening skills.

What is "chaff" anyway?

I'm sure you've observed in your classes that some people are constantly taking notes. Others end up with two lines on one page. Most of us fall in between.

The person who never stops taking notes is either writing a letter to a friend in Iowa or has absolutely no idea what *is* or is *not* important.

The results are dozens of pages of notes (by the end of the semester) that may or may not be helpful. This person is so busy writing that he isn't prepared or even aware that he can ask and answer questions to help himself understand the material better. To use that old adage, he can't see the forest for the trees. He is probably the same person who takes a marking pen and underlines or highlights every word in the book.

Contrast him to the person who thinks note-taking isn't cool, so he only writes down today's date and the homework assignment. He may write something when the teacher says, "Now, write this down and remember it," but he probably just scribbles some nonsense words. After all, he's cool.

Watch him sweat when it's time to study for the exam. He's stuck with a faulty memory and a textbook that may not contain half the material that will be on the test.

Taking concise, clear notes is first and foremost the practice of discrimination—developing your ability to separate the essential from the superfluous, the key concepts, key facts, key ideas from all the rest. In turn, this requires the ability to listen to what your teacher is saying and copying down only what you need to in order to understand the concept. For some, that could mean a single sentence. For others, a detailed example will be the key.

Just remember: The quality of your notes usually has little to do with their *length*—three key lines that reveal the core concepts of a whole lecture are far more valuable than paragraphs of less important data.

Even if you find yourself wandering helplessly in the lecturer's wake, so unsure of what she's saying that you can't begin to separate the important, noteworthy material from the nonessential verbiage, use the techniques discussed in this chapter to organize and condense your notes anyway.

Tkng grt nts in clss

You *know* the year Columbus "discovered" America. You *know* the chemical formula for oxygen. You also *know* Hemingway wrote *The Old Man and the Sea*. So why waste time and space writing them down?

Frequently, your teacher presents material that is commonly known in order to set the stage for further discussion or to introduce material that is more difficult. Don't be so conditioned to copy dates, vocabulary, terms, and names, that you mindlessly scribble down information you already know.

Remember, taking effective notes requires five separate actions on your part:

1. *Listening* actively;
2. *Selecting* pertinent information;
3. *Condensing* it;
4. *Sorting*/organizing it;
5. *Interpreting* it (later).

Develop your shorthand skills

You don't have to be a master of shorthand to stream-line your note-taking. Here are five ways:

1. Eliminate vowels. As a sign that was ubiquitous in the New York City subways used to proclaim, "If u cn rd ths, u cn gt a gd jb." ("If you can read this, you can get a good job.")
2. Use word beginnings ("rep" for representative) and other easy-to-remember abbreviations.
3. Stop putting periods after all abbreviations. (They add up!)
4. Use standard symbols in place of words. Here is a list that will help you in most of your classes (you may recognize many of these symbols from math and logic):

```
┌─────────────────────────────────────────────────┐
│              Standard shorthand symbols           │
│                                                   │
│   ≈        approximately                          │
│   w/       with                                   │
│   w/o      without                                │
│   wh/      which                                  │
│   →        resulting in                           │
│   ←        as a result of/consequence of          │
│   +        and or also                            │
│   *        most importantly                       │
│   cf       compare; in comparison; in relation to │
│   ff       following                              │
│   <        less than                              │
│   >        more than                              │
│   =        the same as                            │
│   ↑        increasing                             │
│   ↓        decreasing                             │
│   esp      especially                             │
│   Δ        change                                 │
│   ⊂        it follows that                        │
│   ∴        therefore                              │
│   ∵        because                                │
└─────────────────────────────────────────────────┘
```

5. Create your own symbols and abbreviations based on your needs and comfort level.

There are three specific symbols I think you'll want to create—they'll be needed again and again:

(W) That's my symbol for "*what?*", as in "What the heck does that mean?" "What did she say?" or "What happened? I'm completely lost!" It denotes something that's been missed—leave space in your notes to fill in the missing part of the puzzle after class.

(M) That's my symbol for "my idea" or "my thought." I want to clearly separate my own thoughts during a lecture from the professor's — include too many of your own ideas (without noting that they *are* yours) and your notes begin to lose some serious value!

(T!) My symbol for "Test!" as in "I'm betting the farm this point is probably on the test, dummy, so don't forget to review it!!!"

Feel free to use your own code for these three important instances; you certainly don't have to use mine.

While I recommend using all the "common" symbols and abbreviations listed previously *all* the time, in *every* class, in order to maintain consistency, you may want to create specific symbols or abbreviations for each class. In chemistry, for example, "TD" may stand for thermodynamics, "K" for the Kinetic Theory of Gases (but don't mix it up with the "K" for Kelvin). In history, "GW" is the father of our country, "ABE" is Mr. Honesty, and "FR" could be French Revolution (or "freedom rider").

How do you keep everything straight? No matter what, summarize your abbreviations of each class's notes, perhaps on the front page in a corner, or create a list on the first page of that class's notebook or binder section for the abbreviations and symbols you intend to use regularly through the semester.

Expanding on your "shorthand"

While you're listening to your instructor, you should be thinking about what you write down. Lectures are filled with so many words that will not be at all helpful when you sit down to study for the big exam. Writing *those* words down and missing some of the truly important points of the lecture is counterproductive: Your notes may look impressively complete, but what are they completely full of? All the important stuff or...?

I've also noticed that many students are prone to write *big* when they are writing fast and to use only a portion of the width of their paper. I guess they figure that turning over pages quickly means they are taking great notes. All it really means is that they are taking notes that will be difficult to read or use when it's review time. Force yourself to write small and take advantage of the entire width of your note paper.

But is it good for *you*?

Do you think this sort of shorthand will work for you? You probably won't at first. When I worked as a reporter, I found that I couldn't trust my notes, at least not at first. But in trying to write so much down I also discovered that I just couldn't trust my note-*taking*. As I gained more experience, however, my note-taking became more and more productive.

Just be careful—in your fervor to adopt my shorthand system, don't abbreviate so much that your notes are absolutely unintelligible to you almost as soon as you write them!

The point here is that you must come up with a note-taking shorthand system that makes sense to *you*. You may certainly choose to abbreviate less and write a little more. Whatever system you develop, just make sure it serves the right purpose: giving you the time to really *listen* to your instructors, rather than only furiously scribbling down what they say.

Draw your way to good grades

The one problem with this whole note-taking system I've discussed is that many people find it more difficult to remember words rather than pictures, especially those who, on the "My Ideal Study Environment" chart in Chapter 2, claimed they received information best visually rather than orally.

Problem solved: *Mapping* is another way to take notes that stresses a more visual style—drawing or diagramming your notes rather than just writing them down.

Let me show you how to map the first few pages of this chapter as an example. Start with a clean sheet of paper and, boxed or circled in the center, write the main topic.

How do you want your picture to read—top to bottom, bottom to top, clockwise in a circle, counterclockwise? I'm going to set mine up top to bottom. After deciding on the first major topic ("Utilizing skills depends on class format") and placing it on your map, add the detail:

The second major topic ("Know your teacher") and those that follow take their place in the line or circle you've chosen, in the direction you've chosen. I've completed a map containing four major topics on page 136.

> How to excel in class

Lectures (emphases: listening, note-taking)

Discussions (emphases: asking/answering, analyzing, discussing)

Combination (emphases: as above)

Hands-on (emphases: development/application of pertinent skills)

> Utilizing skills depends on class format

Active participation: "Grade A" approach

In many nonlecture classes, you will find that discussion, mostly in the form of questions and answers, is actively encouraged. This dialogue serves to both confirm your knowledge and comprehension of specific subject matter and to identify those areas in which you need work.

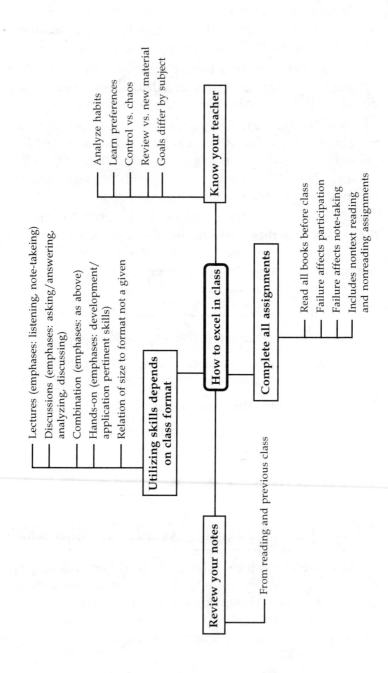

Know your teacher
- Analyze habits
- Learn preferences
- Control *vs.* chaos
- Review vs. new material
- Goals differ by subject

Utilizing skills depends on class format
- Lectures (emphases: listening, note-taking)
- Discussions (emphases: asking/answering, analyzing, discussing)
- Combination (emphases: as above)
- Hands-on (emphases: development/application pertinent skills)
- Relation of size to format not a given

How to excel in class

Complete all assignments
- Read all books before class
- Failure affects participation
- Failure affects note-taking
- Includes nontext reading and nonreading assignments

Review your notes
- From reading and previous class

Whatever the format in which you find yourself, participate in any discussion to the best of your ability. Most teachers consider class participation a key ingredient in your semester grades. No matter how many papers and tests you "ace," if you never open your mouth in class, you shouldn't be surprised to get less than an A.

If you're having trouble following an argument or particular line of thought, ask for a review or for clarification.

Don't ask questions or make points looking to impress your teacher—your real motive will probably be pretty obvious. Remember what you *are* there for—to master the material.

Based on the professor's preferences and the class format, ask the questions you feel need answers.

Be careful you don't innocently distract yourself from practicing your now-excellent note-taking skills by starting to analyze something you don't understand or, worse, creating mental arguments because you disagree with something your teacher or a classmate said. Taking the time to mentally frame an elaborate question is equally distracting. All three cause the same problem: *You're not listening!*

Finally, listen closely to the words of your classmates. Knowledge has no boundaries, and you'll often find their comments, attitudes, and opinions as helpful and insightful as your instructor's.

What if you're shy or just get numb whenever you're called on? Ask a question rather than taking part in the discussion—it's easier and, over time, may help you break the ice and jump into the discussion. If you really can't open your mouth without running a fever, consider taking a public speaking course.

Most importantly, prepare and practice. Fear of standing in front of a class or even participating from the safety of your seat is, for many of you, really a symptom of lack of confidence.

And *lack of confidence stems from lack of preparation.* The more prepared you are—if you know the material backwards and forwards—the more likely you will be able to, even *want* to, raise your hand and "strut your stuff." Practicing with friends, parents, or relatives may also help.

If you are having trouble with oral reports, they are covered separately in Chapter 7. I think you'll find the hints I've included there will eliminate a lot of the fear such talks seem to engender.

What to do *after* class

As soon as possible after your class, review your notes, fill in the "blanks," mark down questions you need to research in your text or ask during the next class, and remember to mark any new assignments on your weekly calendar.

I tend to discourage recopying your notes as a general practice, since I believe it's more important to work on taking good notes the first time around and not waste the time it takes to recopy. *But* if you tend to write fast and illegibly, it might also be a good time to rewrite your notes so they're readable, taking the opportunity to summarize as you go. The better your notes, the better your chance of capturing and recalling the pertinent material.

This is why I recommend "one period on, one off." Schedule an open period, even a half hour, after each class to review that class's notes and prepare for the next one. It is not easy for most high school students to do so, but in college you have a greater say in scheduling your classes.

CHAPTER 6

How to Use Your Library

LIBRARIES CONTAIN THE written record of humankind's brief stay on Planet Earth. They stand unparalleled as one of our finest accomplishments and unchallenged as reference and research sources. In your attempt to develop lifelong study skills, you will find yourself using the library constantly. It presents a single well from which we can draw knowledge and material throughout our lifetimes...without ever worrying about coming up dry.

Libraries are a staple in cities and small towns across the United States and represent an amazingly democratic aspect of our culture. Rules and restrictions vary from library to library — public vs. college, large vs. small — but high school and college students usually have access to virtually all library materials. Don't forget the best part: These services are *free*. A library card is your ticket to the world of knowledge that could keep you busy for the rest of your life.

Where to find a library

Start with your local phone directory. I can virtually guarantee there is a library within minutes of your home, since there are more than 15,000 public and nearly 5,000 academic (high school, college, university, and graduate school) libraries in the United States. These are the ones you would most likely be using.

If for some reason you don't think the resources of these nearly 20,000 libraries are sufficient, there are also nearly 500 libraries on military bases throughout the country, plus more than 10,000 government and special (law, medical, religious, art) libraries nationwide.

And, of course, you can access nearly any library in the world from the comfort of your own home. All you need is a computer, a modem, and some Net-surfing smarts.

Many major university libraries dwarf all but the largest public library systems. Harvard, Yale, Princeton, and similar bastions of learning offer tremendous resources even the major public libraries can't. If you have access to a major university library, consider it your good fortune and take advantage of it.

How libraries work

Most libraries are divided into reading rooms, restricted collections, and unrestricted book stacks. Unrestricted book stacks are those through which anyone using the library can wander, choosing books to use while in the library or, if allowed, to take home. Restricted areas generally include any special collections of rare books, those open only to scholars or to those with particular credentials, either by library rule or by order of whoever donated the collection (and, often, the room housing it). In some libraries, *all* book stacks are closed, and *all* books must be obtained from a librarian.

Most libraries contain both *circulating materials* — those books and other items you may check out and take home with you — and *non-circulating materials* — those that must be used only in the library. All fiction, general nonfiction, and even most scholarly titles will usually be found in the first group. Reference material, periodicals, and books in special collections are usually in the second.

How your library is organized

To provide organization and facilitate access, most libraries utilize the Dewey Decimal Classification System, which uses numbers from 000 to 999 to classify all material by subject matter. It begins by organizing all books into 10 major groupings:

000 - 099	General
100 - 199	Philosophy
200 - 299	Religion
300 - 399	Social Sciences
400 - 499	Language
500 - 599	Natural Science and Mathematics
600 - 699	Technology
700 - 799	Fine Arts
800 - 899	Literature
900 - 999	General Geography and History

Given the millions of books available in major libraries, just dividing them into these 10 groups would still make it quite difficult to find a specific title. So each of the 10 major groupings is further divided into 10 and each of these 100 groups is assigned to more specific subjects within each large group. For example, within the Philosophy classification (100), 150 is psychology and 170 is ethics. Within the history classification (900), 910 is travel and 930 is ancient history.

There is even further subdivision. Mathematics is given its own number in the 500 (Science) series—510. But specific subjects within mathematics are further classified: 511 is arithmetic, 512 is algebra, and so on.

Finally, to simplify your search for materials even more, the last two digits in the Dewey Decimal code signify the type of book:

01 Philosophy of
02 Outlines of
03 Dictionary of
04 Essays about
05 Periodicals on
06 Society transactions and proceedings
07 Study or teaching of
08 Collections
09 History of

If your library doesn't use the Dewey system, it probably is organized according to the Library of Congress System, which uses letters instead of numbers to denote major categories:

A   General works (encyclopedias and other reference)
B   Philosophy, Psychology, and Religion
C   History: Auxiliary sciences (archeology, genealogy, and so on)
D   History: General, non-American
E   American history (general)
F   American history (local)

G Geography/Anthropology
H Social sciences (sociology, business, economics)
J   Political sciences
K Law
L   Education
M Music
N Fine arts (art and architecture)
P Language/Literature
Q Sciences
R Medicine
S Agriculture
T Technology
U Military science
V Naval science
Z Bibliography/Library science

There are more than 50,000 new books published each year, and your library probably buys a number of these. Books arrive almost daily and are sent to the cataloging section for classification, special bindings (if needed), and shelf placement. Once entered into the system, books are indexed in the card catalog (or, as is more and more often the case, in the computer) by author, title, and subject matter. Finding a biography of Tolstoy, for example, is as easy as looking up Tolstoy in the card catalog and copying down the appropriate codes for the particular one you want. (Yes, your library probably has more than one!)

In a closed-shelf environment, you would give the appropriate numbers to a librarian and the books would be delivered to you. If the shelves are open, you have merely to learn the way they are organized and go search for your own books. Open shelf areas are often designated by letters of the alphabet (for fiction), by subject matter (in smaller libraries), or, in virtually all major libraries, according to the Dewey or Library of Congress codes.

Where to start

In your elementary school days, you probably relied on one of the tried and true encyclopedias—*World Book*, *Britannica*, *Grolier's*, *Collier's*—when you had to write a report. While such broad reference works are still a reasonable starting point (though you'll probably be consulting them online), there are a surprising number of topic-specific encyclopedias, dictionaries, and almanacs available in many libraries. While a college-level paper may well require significant additional research, many high school students will find a large amount of research material in just one of these resources.

From a recent issue of *Library Journal*, the trade magazine for librarians, here's a sampling of new reference works published just in the last year: *Encyclopedia of Christmas*, *Charlie Chan Film Encyclopedia*, *Encyclopedia of Paleontology*, *Encyclopedia of the Renaissance*, *Dictionary of Theology*, *A History of Women's Writing in France*, *Encyclopedia of Deserts*, *Encyclopedia of the Solar System*, *Encyclopedia of Human Nutrition*, *Encyclopedia of Smoking and Tobacco*, *Historical Encyclopedia of Nursing*, and *Oxford Companion to Food*.

Needless to say, there was an equally impressive list of newly available CD-ROMs and new reference Web sites. These many current resources should make it increasingly easy to choose a good topic, establish a reasonable thesis, and gather enough information to construct an initial outline, without having to do any further research.

But unless you *are* still in elementary school, completing an "A+" paper will necessitate turning to other sources for more detailed information.

Feeling overwhelmed by the stacks of volumes, classification systems, card catalogs, and computers? You still have no excuse for not taking advantage of your library. All you have to do—if at all confused about tracking down the information you need—is ask the librarian.

Where to look for materials

You should review as wide a variety of reference materials as possible.

But how do you find out whether anyone has written a magazine or newspaper article about your topic? How do you know if there are any government documents or pamphlets that might be of help? How do you locate those written-by-the-experts reference books?

Look in your library's publication and online indexes. These indexes list all of the articles, books, and other materials that have been published and/or are available in your library.

I've listed some of the major publication indexes below. There are many, many others, so remember to ask your librarian for additional suggestions.

1. **The card catalog.** This is a list of all the books in your library. (Although many libraries now store it on computer, it's still often called a card catalog because it used to be kept on index cards.) Books are indexed in three different ways: by subject, by author, and by title. Some libraries have card catalogs that list all books available — whether at your library or somewhere else. If another library has the books, often your librarian can get them for you. This is called Inter-Library Loan and is very common at the college level.

2. **Book catalogs.** The best-known of these are _Books in Print, Forthcoming Books_, and the _Cumulative Book Index_.

3. **Periodical indexes.** To find out if any magazine articles have been published on your subject, go to a periodical index. _The Readers' Guide to_

Periodical Literature, which indexes articles published in the most popular American magazines, may be one with which you're familiar.

4. **Vertical file.** Here's where you'll find pamphlets and brochures.

5. **Guide to U.S. Government Publications, American Statistical Index,** and **Congressional Information Service Index.** These are all useful for locating government publications.

6. **Computer databases**. Widely used indexes are available covering American and world history, art, biology, philosophy, religion, psychology, engineering, and much more.

7. **The Internet**. Most magazines, newspapers, encyclopedias, government organizations, and so forth have Web sites that can be a starting point for your search. They often have links to other sites where you can find full-length articles and stories, biographic information, and the like. A word of caution about Internet resources: Make sure your sources are credible. Anyone can post information on the Web, whether they're qualified or not, whether the material is accurate or not. Make sure your sources are reputable so your teacher doesn't question the validity of your information.

Your approach to research

All of us who have become familiar with the wonders of the library have probably developed our own approach to enjoying its amenities and using them most efficiently.

My own experience emphasizes what may already be obvious: Getting the right start is all important. Since I try to keep from becoming overwhelmed with material, I start any research working with the broadest outlines or topics (and the broadest resources) and wind my way down the ladder, getting more and more specific in topic and sources as I go:

1. Consult any of the numerous leading **encyclopedias** you will find in your library — _Britannica, Americana, Collier's, World Book,_ and so forth. Here you'll find an overview and historical perspective on the area. Encyclopedic entries are usually the most comprehensive and concise you will find. They cover so much territory and are so (relatively) up-to-date that they are an ideal "big-picture" resource. And don't forget to seek out a subject-specific encyclopedia like those we discussed a little earlier. If you are writing a paper about a historical or contemporary figure, also consider skimming a biographical dictionary or, even better, one of the specific volumes in the _Who's Who_ series, which ranges from _Who's Who in Art_ and _Who's Who in American Jewry_ to _Who's Who in Vietnam_ and _Who's Who in Theatre._

2. With overview in hand, you can start consulting the **major indexes and directories** your library has to develop a list of more specific resources. Obviously, the entries in these major resources can then be directly consulted — specific issues of _The New York Times_ on microfilm, periodicals at the periodicals desk, and so on. In no time at all, you'll develop a long list of names and places to check out, leading you to a number of potential topics and sources.

Think you'll run out of sources?

In one brief tour of your library's resources, you'll easily discover and know how to obtain more material than you would need to write a book on virtually any one of the subtopics, let alone a report encompassing all of them.

What if you're uncomfortable in the library? An infrequent user? Or simply find it a confusing place that's more trouble than it's worth? As I've emphasized, developing *any* habit is just a matter of practice. The more you use the library, the more comfortable you will become using it, and the more books you'll become comfortable with. In a very short time, you will have your own list of resources that you start with whenever you receive an assignment.

Many of you might not use the library as much as you should (or even would like) because it seems like a confusing series of catacombs. The more comfortable you are—the more you know about the materials it contains and how to locate and use them—the more you will *want* to be there.

And the more help you will be able to obtain from this great resource that's just waiting to welcome you!

Surf's up!

In 1988, when I wrote the first edition of this book, I composed it, formatted it, and printed it on (gasp) a personal computer. Yes, boys and girls, in those halcyon days, I was surfing a wave that didn't hit shore for a few more years. Most people did *not* have a computer, yet alone a neighborhood network and DSL, or surf the Web (whatever that was), or chat online, or Instant Message their friends, or…you get the point.

In case you've been living in a cave that Bill Gates forgot to wire, those days are very dead and gone. And you should cheer, even if you aren't sure what DOS was (is? could be?). Because the spread of the personal computer and, even more, the Internet, have taken studying from the Dark Ages to the Info Age in merely a decade.

The Internet has absolutely revolutionized research. Whether you're writing a paper, putting together a reading list, studying for the SAT, or just trying to organize your life, it has become a more valuable tool than the greatest library in the world. Heck, it _is_ the greatest library in the world...and more. So if you are not Internet savvy (yes, I'm talking to the parents out there, couldn't you tell?), admit you're a dummy, buy a book (over the Internet, of course), and get wired. You'll be missing far too much — and be studying far harder — without it.

There's no room in this book to list even a smattering of pertinent Internet sites. Wherever you go on the Net, just remember:

- Some of the sites are informative and well-organized, some are quirky and skimpy.

- Some are well-researched and trustworthy, and some are the rantings of a mad person. Just because you see it on your computer screen doesn't mean that it's the truth.

- Some provide unbiased information with no ulterior motive, some slant their information to sell you on their cause. Some are just offering enough information to entice you to buy something.

- Some are easy to use, some require you to search through listings to find what you need.

- Some have the information, some link you to other sites, and some are simply listings of sites.

- Some may be gone when you look for them again. That happens.

- Some are free, but some cost, and cost a lot. Be sure to check out cost before going online.

Despite the immensity and importance of the Internet's resources, brick-and-mortar libraries are certainly not dinosaurs. Just because you can visit nearly any library in the world without leaving your computer screen is no reason to avoid becoming intimately familiar with your local or school library. You will find that doing *some* things online is not always as interesting, efficient, or fun as doing them "in person." Libraries are a special place.

CHAPTER 7

How to Write Terrific Papers

IT'S GOING TO happen. Whether you like it or not. Sooner or later, you'll have to prepare written and/or oral reports for virtually every one of your classes. And if you're like most students, your reaction will be the same every time: "Why me? What do I do? Where do I start?"

Reading this chapter will not make you such a good writer that you can quit school and start visiting bookstores to preen in front of the window displays featuring your latest best-seller.

But there is absolutely no reason to fear a written paper or oral report, once you know the simple steps to take and rules to follow to complete it satisfactorily. Once you realize that 90 percent of preparing a paper has *nothing* to do with writing...or even being *able* to write. And once you're confident that preparing papers by following my suggestions will probably get you a grade or two higher than you've gotten before...even if you think you are the world's poorest excuse for a writer.

Doing a research paper requires a lot of work. But the payoff is great, too. You will learn, for example:

1. How to track down information about *any* subject.
2. How to sort through that information and come to a conclusion about your subject.
3. How to prepare an organized, in-depth report.
4. How to communicate your ideas clearly and effectively.

Once you develop these skills, you'll be able to apply them in *all* your high school or college classes, not only when you prepare other research papers, but also when you tackle smaller assignments, such as essays and oral reports.

When you graduate, these same skills will help you get ahead in the work world; the ability to analyze a subject and communicate through the written word are keys to success, no matter what career you choose.

Of all the things you'll learn in school, the skills you acquire as we produce your research paper will be among the most valuable.

5 basic rules of paper-writing

Let's start with the fundamental rules that need to be emblazoned on your wall:

1. **Always** follow your teacher's directions to the letter.
2. **Always** hand in your paper on time.

3. **Always** hand in a clean and clear copy of your paper.

4. **Never** allow a spelling or grammatical error in your paper.

5. **Always** keep at least one copy of every paper you write.

You wanted it *type*written?

Your teacher's directions may include:

✎ A general subject area from which topics should be chosen—"some aspect of Lincoln's presidency," "a 19th-century invention," or "a poem by Wordsworth."

✎ Specific requirements regarding format—typed, double-spaced, include title page, do not include title page, whatever.

✎ Suggested length—for example, 10 to 15 typewritten pages.

✎ Other requirements—turn in general outline before topic is approved; get verbal okay on topic before proceeding; don't include quotes (from other works) longer than a single paragraph, other idiosyncrasies of your own teachers.

Whatever his or her directions, follow them *to the letter*. High school teachers may be somewhat forgiving, but I have known college professors who simply refused to accept a paper that was not prepared *exactly* as they instructed—and gave the poor but wiser student an F for it (without even *reading* it).

At some point, you'll undoubtedly run into a teacher or professor who gives few or no instructions at all. You ask, "How long?", she says, "As long as it takes." Use your common sense. If you're in junior high school or high school, I doubt she is seeking a 50-page novella. Likewise, if you're in college, it's unlikely any of your professors think a three-page paper is "as long as it takes." Use previous assignments as a guide. Follow the suggestions on page 155. If in doubt, try again to pin down an answer.

If you are unsure of a specific requirement or if the suggested area of topics is unclear, it is *your* responsibility to talk to your teacher and clarify whatever points are confusing you.

It is also not a bad idea to choose two or three topics you'd like to write about and seek his or her preliminary approval if the assignment seems particularly vague — this way, you'll *know* for sure that you are fulfilling the topic requirement.

So then my dog chewed the paper...

Since you've studied and memorized Chapter 4, there is certainly no reason, short of catastrophic illness or life-threatening emergency, for you to *ever* be late with an assignment. Again, some teachers will refuse to accept a paper that is late. At best, they will mark you down for your lateness, perhaps turning an A paper into a B...or worse. In the case of legitimate extenuating circumstances (extended illness, death in the family, and so on), let your teacher know immediately and arrange for an extension.

Is that jelly stain worth a B?

Teachers have to read a lot of papers and shouldn't be faulted for being human if, after hundreds of pages, they come upon your jelly-stained, pencil-written tome and get a bit discouraged. Nor should you be surprised if they give you a lower grade than the content might merit just because the presentation is so poor.

I am not advocating "form over substance." Far from it—the content is what the teacher is looking for, and he or she will be basing your grade primarily on *what* you write. But presentation is important. So follow these simple rules:

- Never handwrite your paper.

- If you use a word processor or a word-processing program on your computer, use a new ribbon in your dot matrix printer and/or check the toner cartridge in your laser printer. If you type (or have someone else type) your paper, use clean white bond and (preferably) a new carbon ribbon so that the images are crisp and clear.

- Unless otherwise instructed, always double-space a typewritten paper.

- Use a simple typeface that is clear and easy-to-read; avoid those that are too big—stretching a five-page paper to 10—or too small and hard to read.

- Never use a fancy italic, modern, or any other ornate or hard-to-read typeface for the entire paper.

Use your old papers as maps

There should be a number of helpful messages in your returned papers, which is why it's so important to retain them. What did your teacher have to say? Are there comments applicable to the paper you're writing now—poor writing, lack of organization, lack of research, bad transitions between paragraphs, poor grammar or punctuation, misspellings? The more such comments—and, one would expect, the lower the grade—the more extensive the "map" your teacher has given you for your *next* paper, showing you right where to "locate" your A.

If you got a low grade but there aren't any comments, shouldn't you have asked the teacher why you got such a poor grade? You may get the comments you need to make the next paper better. You will also be showing the teacher you actually care, which could help your grade the next time around.

Many employers merrily use resumes and cover letters with grammatical and/or spelling errors for hoops practice. Don't expect your teachers to be any more forgiving—there are definitely a few out there who will award an F without even noticing that the rest of the paper is great; it's too bad you misspelled "Constantinople" or left a participle twisting slowly in the wind.

The Fry paper-writing system

The more complex a task or the longer you need to complete it, the more important your organization becomes. By breaking down any paper-writing project into a series of manageable steps, you'll start to feel less chaotic, hectic, and afraid right away.

Here are the steps that, with some minor variations along the way, are common to virtually any written report or paper:

1. Research potential topics.
2. Finalize topic.
3. Carry out initial library research.
4. Prepare general outline.
5. Do detailed library research.
6. Prepare detailed outline (from note cards).
7. Write first draft.
8. Do additional research (if necessary).
9. Write second draft.
10. Spell-check and proofread.

11. Have someone *else* proofread.
12. Produce final draft.
13. Proofread one last time.
14. Turn it in and collect your A+.

Create a work schedule

Get out your calendar. Find the date on which your paper is due. How many weeks do you have till then? Plan to spend at least half of that time on research, the other half on writing.

Now, block out set periods of time during each week to work on your paper. Schedule two- or three-hour chunks of work time, rather than many short periods, so you can really immerse yourself in your work.

As you make up your work schedule, set deadlines for completing various steps of your paper. For example:

Week 1:	Decide on topic and "angle" of your paper.
Week 2:	Make list of references.
Weeks 3/4:	Read reference materials; take notes.
Weeks 5/6:	Do detailed outline; write first draft.
Week 7:	Edit paper; prepare bibliography.
Week 8:	Proofread paper; type final copy.

You should probably plan on consulting and/or taking notes from at least 10 different books, articles, or other reference materials. (Your teacher or subject may require more.) And you should plan on writing two or three drafts of your paper before you arrive at the final copy.

Refer to your work schedule often, and adjust your speed if you find yourself lagging behind.

Steps 1 and 2:
Consider and choose topics

In some cases, your teacher will assign your topic. In others, your teacher will assign a general area of study, but you will have the freedom to pick a specific topic within that general area.

There are some pitfalls you must avoid. Let's say you need to write a 15-page paper for your government class, and you decide your topic will be "Disability-Related Legislation in American History." Can you really cover that in 15 pages? Not unless you simply rehash the high points, *à la* your third-grade history book. You could write *volumes* on the subject (many people have!) and have plenty left to say.

Instead, you need to focus on a particular, limited angle of your subject, such as, "The Passage of the ADA (Americans with Disabilities Act)."

By the same token, you must not get too narrow in your focus. Choose a subject that's too limited, and you might run out of things to say on the second page of your paper. "The Chapman Amendment to the ADA" might make an interesting one- or two-page essay, but it won't fill 10 or 15 pages.

Pick a topic that's too obscure, and you may find that little or no information has been written about it. In which case, you will have to conduct your own experiments, interview your own research subjects, and come up with your own original data. Hint: If you can't find a single *book* on your supposed topic, rethink it! While you could choose a topic that can be researched via magazine articles, the newspaper, monographs, and the like, why make your life so difficult if you don't have to?

Make sure there is enough research material available about your topic. And make sure that there are enough _different_ sources of material — different authors, different books, and so forth — so you can get a well-rounded view of your subject (and not be forced for lack of other material to find ways to make somebody else's points sound like your own).

Taking all of the above into consideration, do a little brainstorming now about possible topics for your paper. Don't stop with the first idea — come up with several different possibilities. Put this book down until you have a list of three or four potential topics.

How about trying to get two or more papers for two or more classes _out of the same research?_ You may not be able to simply produce one paper for two classes, but with a little extra research — _not_ what you would need to do for an entirely different paper — you may well utilize a good portion of the first paper as the basis for a second. What a great way to maximize your library time!

Step 3: Begin initial library research

Got your list? Then get thee to a library. You need to do a little advance research. Scan your library's card-catalog index and _Readers' Guide to Periodical Literature_ or other publication indexes. See how many books and articles have been written about each topic on your "possibilities" list. Next, read a short background article or encyclopedia entry about each topic.

Alternatively, spend a little time online. Are there specific Web sites devoted to your topic? Lucky you! Or does a keyword search result in 10,424 matches, none of which have a _thing_ to do with your topic?

With any luck at all, you should be left with at least one topic that looks like a good research subject. If two or more topics passed your preliminary-research test, pick the one that interests you most. You're going to spend a lot of time learning about your subject. There's no rule that says you can't enjoy it!

Develop a temporary thesis

Once you have chosen the topic for your paper, you must develop a temporary thesis. (The word "thesis" is a relative of "hypothesis" and means about the same thing—the central argument you will attempt to prove or disprove in your paper. A thesis is not the same thing as a *topic*. Your topic is what you study; your thesis is the conclusion you draw from that study.)

A "thesis statement" sums up the main point of your paper. It's generally just a sentence or two.

Note that I said *temporary* thesis. It may not wind up being your final thesis. Because you haven't completed all your research yet, you can only come up with a "best-guess" thesis at this point.

If a temporary thesis doesn't spring easily to mind—and it probably won't—sit back and do some more brainstorming. Ask yourself questions like:

- What's special or unusual about ____? (Fill in the blank with your topic.)

- How is ____ related to events in the past?

- What impact has ____ made on society?

- What do I want the world to know about ____?

- What questions do I have about ____?

You may discover during this preliminary research phase that your temporary thesis just won't fly. You may have to revise it, perhaps even settling on a thesis that's the exact opposite of your original! In fact, you may have to revise your thesis several times during the course of your research.

Step 4: Create a temporary outline

Once you have developed your temporary thesis, give some thought as to how you might approach the subject in your paper. Jot down the various issues you plan to investigate. Then, come up with a brief, temporary outline of your paper, showing the order in which you might discuss those issues.

Don't worry too much about this outline — it will be brief, at best. It's simply a starting point for your research, a plan of attack. But don't skip this step, either — it will be a big help in organizing your research findings.

Step 5: Do detailed library research

We've already reviewed the library and online resources and how to take advantage of them. Now, let's talk about exactly how you'll keep track of all the resources and information you'll gather for your paper.

To create your working bibliography, you'll need a supply of 3 x 5 index cards. You'll also use index cards when you take notes for your paper, so buy a big batch now. About 300 cards ought to suffice. While you're at it, pick up one of those little file boxes designed to hold the cards. Put your name, address, and phone number on the file. If you lose it, some kind stranger can (and hopefully will) return it.

Before you do anything else, send away for anything you want to review that isn't available in your library. If you want a brochure from a particular association, for example, order it now. It may take a few weeks for such materials to arrive. (Check the Internet to see if any needed material can be easily downloaded. The more skilled Web browsers among you may spend little on postage, even for obscure material from Zimbabwe.)

Start a systematic search for any materials that might have information related to your paper. Look through the indexes we covered in Chapter 6 and any other indexes your librarian recommends. (And don't overlook the extensive resources available online.)

When you find a book, article, or other resource that looks promising, take out a blank note card. On the front of the card, write down the following information:

In the upper right-hand corner of the card: The library call number (Dewey decimal number or Library of Congress number), if there is one. Add any other details that will help you locate the material on the library shelves ("Science Reading Room," "Reference Room").

On the main part of the card: The author's name, if given — last name first, first name, middle name/initial. Then the title of the article, if applicable, in quotation marks. Then the name of the book, magazine, newspaper, or other publication — underlined.

Add any details you will need if you have to find the book or article again, such as the date of publication, edition, volume number, and page numbers on which the article or information appears.

In the upper left-hand corner of the card: Number it. The first card you write will be #1, the second, #2, and so on. If you happen to mess up and skip a number somewhere along the line, don't worry. It's only important that you assign a different number to each card.

At the bottom of the card: If you're going to be researching in more than one library, write the library's name. Also write down the name of the index in which you found the resource, in case you need to refer to it again.

Do this for *each* potential source of information you find. *And put only one resource on each card.*

Citing online information

Because students are increasingly using online sources, the MLA and APA, which publish style guides for research papers, have integrated electronic citations into their latest editions. Other good sources include _Bibliographic Formats for Citing Electronic Information_ by Nancy B. Crane and Xia

Sample bibliography card for a book

```
(1)                                              315.6
                                    Main Reading Room


                       Spechler, Jay W.
   Reasonable Accommodation: Profitable Compliance with the
                 Americans with Disabilities Act
                      (see esp. pp. 54-61)

                    ComputerCard Catalog
                       College Library
```

Sample bibliography card for a magazine article

```
(2)                                         Periodical Room


                       Smolowe, Jill

                 "Noble Aims, Mixed Results"
                           Time
                  (July 31, 1995; pp. 54-55)

                       Readers' Guide
                       College Library
```

Sample bibliography card for a newspaper article

```
(3)                                           Microfiche Room


                        Wade, Betsy

                  "Disabled Access to Inns at Issue"
                        The New York Times
                  (April 14, 1996, section 5, page 4)

                      New York Times Index
                  Franklin Lakes Public Library

```

Li (Meckler Media) and *Online: A Reference Guide to Using Online Resources* by Andrew Harnack and Eugene Kepplinger (Bedford/St. Martin's). Both books have excerpts available online. Sample online citation:

Furfaro, John P. and Maury B. Josephson. "Reasonable Accommodation to Disability Act." New York Law Journal. http://homepages.go.com/~atlanticcity/040299c4.htm(2 April 1999)

Now hit the books

Set aside solid blocks of time for your library work. It's better to schedule a handful of extended trips to the library than 15 or 20 brief visits. When you go to the library, take your bibliography cards, a good supply of blank index cards, your preliminary outline, and several pens or pencils.

Your bibliography cards serve as the map for your information treasure hunt. Get out a stack of five or six cards, and locate the materials listed on those cards. Set up camp at a secluded desk or table and get to work.

When you write your paper, you'll get all the information you need from your notes, rather than from the original sources. Therefore, it's vital that you take careful and complete notes. What sort of information should you put in your notes? Anything related to your subject and especially to your thesis. This includes:

1. General background information (names, dates, historical data).
2. Research statistics.
3. Quotes by experts.
4. Definitions of technical terms.

You may be used to keeping your notes in a three-ring binder or notepad. I'm going to show you a better way—recording all of your notes on index cards.

Let's say that you have found a reference book that contains some information about your subject. Before you begin taking notes, get out the bibliography card for that book.

Check that all of the information on your card is correct. Is the title exactly as printed on the book? Is the author's name spelled correctly? Add any other information you'll need to include in your final bibliography. (For more information on exactly what you need to include, be sure to refer to the newest edition of *Improve Your Writing.* It includes details on bibliographic and source note formats.)

Note-taking guidelines

Once your bibliography card is finished, set it aside. Get out some blank index cards and start taking notes from your reference source. Follow these guidelines:

 Write one thought, idea, quote, or fact on each card. If you encounter a very long quote or string of data, you can write on both the front and back of a card, if necessary. *But never carry a note to a second card.*

✎ **Write in your own words.** Summarize key points about a paragraph or section. Avoid copying things word for word.

✎ **Put quotation marks around any material copied verbatim.** It's okay to include in your paper a sentence or paragraph written by someone else to emphasize a particular point (providing you do so on a limited basis). But you must copy such statements *exactly as written* in the original source — every word, every comma, every period.

Adding detail to your note cards

As you finish each note card, do the following:

✎ **In the upper left-hand corner of the card,** write down the resource number of the corresponding bibliography card (from its left-hand corner). This will remind you where you got the information.

✎ **Below the resource number,** write the page number(s) on which the information appeared.

✎ **Get out your preliminary outline.** Under which outline topic heading does the information on your card seem to fit? Jot the appropriate topic letter in the upper right-hand corner of your note card.

If you're not sure where the information fits into your outline, put an asterisk instead of a topic letter. Later, when you do a more detailed outline, you can try to fit these "miscellaneous" note cards into specific areas.

✎ **Next to the topic letter,** jot down a one- or two-word "headline" that describes the information on the card.

✎ **When you have finished taking notes from a particular resource**, put a check mark on the bibliography card. This will let you know that you're done with that resource, at least for now.

Be sure that you transfer information accurately to your note cards. Double-check names, dates, and other statistics. As with your bibliography cards, it's not so important that you put each of these elements in the exact places I've outlined above. You just need to be consistent. Always put the page number in the same place, in the same manner. Ditto with the resource number, the topic heading, and the headline.

Add your personal notes

Throughout your note-taking process, you may want to make some "personal" note cards. On these cards, jot down any thoughts, ideas, or impressions you may have about your subject or your thesis.

Write each thought on a separate note card, as you have with information you've taken from other resources. And assign your note card a topic heading and mini-headline, too. In the space where you would normally put the number of the resource, put your own initials.

Sample completed note card

(2)	B
p. 55	unemployment/compliance

2/3 all working-age disabled people still unemployed–same portion jobless when law passed

Step 6: Prepare a detailed outline

Your research is done.

Which means that at least *one-half* of your *paper*—perhaps as much as *three-quarters* of it—is done, even though you've yet to write one word of the first draft.

It's time to organize your data. You need to decide if your temporary thesis is still on target, determine how you will organize your paper, and create a detailed outline.

This is where the note-card system really pays off. Your note cards give you a great tool for organizing your paper. Get out all of your note cards, then:

1. Group together all of the cards that share the same outline topic letter (the letter in the right-hand corner of each card).

2. Put those different groups in order, according to your temporary outline. (Put all of your topic A cards at the front of the stack of cards, followed by topic B cards, then topic C cards, and so on.)

3. Within each topic group, sort the cards even further. Group the cards that share the same "headline" (the two-word title in the upper right-hand corner).

4. Go through your miscellaneous topic cards, the ones you marked with an asterisk. Can you fit any of them into your existing topic groups? If so, replace the asterisk with the topic letter. If not, put the card at the very back of your stack.

Your note cards now should be organized according to your preliminary outline. Take a few minutes to read through your note cards, beginning at the front of the stack and moving through to the back. What you're reading is actually a rough sketch of your paper—the information you've collected in the order you plan to present it in your paper. Does that order make sense? Would another arrangement work better?

Here are some of the different organizational approaches you might consider for your paper:

1. **Chronological.** Discuss events in the order in which they happened (by time of occurrence).
2. **Spatial.** Present information in geographical or physical order (from north to south, largest to smallest).
3. **Cause/effect.** One by one, discuss the effects of a series of individual events or actions.
4. **Problem/solution.** Present a series of problems and possible solutions.
5. **Compare/contrast.** Discuss similarities and differences between people, things, or events.
6. **Order of importance.** Discuss the most important aspects of an issue first and continue through to the least important.

If necessary, revise your general outline according to the organizational decision you have made. Next, go through each group of cards that share the same topic letter. Rearrange them so that they, too, follow the organizational pattern you chose.

After you sort all the cards that have been assigned a specific topic heading (A, B, C), review cards that are marked with an asterisk. Try to figure out where they fit in your stack of cards.

Don't include a card if the information it contains just doesn't seem to fit anywhere. It's possible that the data just isn't relevant to your revised thesis. Set it aside for now. You can try to include it again later.

And while you're setting aside inappropriate notes, don't forget to seek out "holes" in your paper—those areas that cry out for a more up-to-date fact, a good example, a stronger transition. No one likes to discover the need to do a little more research, but if *you've* identified the omission, I guarantee your teacher will notice it. Don't let a "black hole" turn a potentially great paper into one that's merely okay just because you don't want to spend another hour online or in the library.

Now flip through your note cards from front to back. See that? You've created a detailed outline without even knowing it. The topic letters on your note cards match the main topics of your outline. And those headlines on your note cards are the subtopics for your outline.

Simply transfer your note-card headlines to paper. They appear on your outline in the same order as they appear in your stack of cards.

Step 7: Write the first draft

You may not have realized it, but you've already *done* a lot of the hard work that goes into the writing stage. You have thought about how your paper will flow, you have organized your notes, and you have prepared a detailed outline. All that's left is to transfer your information and ideas from note cards to paper.

Good writing takes concentration and thought. And concentration and thought require quiet—and lots of it! You also need to have plenty of desk space, so you can spread out your note cards in front of you, your work area should be well-lit, and you should have a dictionary and thesaurus close at hand. If possible, "write" directly on to a computer, so you can add, delete, and rearrange your words at the touch of a button.

Remember: At this point, your goal is to produce a rough draft—with the emphasis on the word "rough." Your first draft isn't supposed to be perfect. It's *supposed* to need revision.

But your thoughts, ideas, and logic are the foundation of your paper. And you need to build a house's foundation before you worry about hanging the front door. So, for now, just concentrate on getting your thoughts on paper. Don't worry about using exactly the "right" word. Don't worry about getting commas in all the right places. We'll take care of all that polishing later.

Your note cards helped you come up with a detailed outline. Now, they're going to help you plot out the actual paragraphs and sentences of your paper.

1. Your note cards should be arranged in the same order as your detailed outline. Take out all of the note cards labeled with the letter of the first topic on your outline.

2. Out of that stack, take out all the cards marked with the same headline as the first subheading in your outline.

3. Look at the information on those cards. Think about how the various pieces of information might fit together in a paragraph.

4. Rearrange those cards so they fall in the order you have determined is best for the paragraph.

5. Do this for each group of cards, until you reach the end of the deck.

Each paragraph in your paper is like a mini-essay. It should have a topic sentence — a statement of the key point or fact you will discuss in the paragraph — and contain the evidence to support it. This evidence can come in different forms, such as quotes from experts, research statistics, examples from research or from your own experience, detailed descriptions, or other background information.

Stack up your paragraphs like bricks into your own "wall of evidence." Construct each paragraph carefully, and your readers will have no choice but to agree with your final conclusion.

If paragraphs are the bricks, transitions — a sentence or phrase that moves the reader from one thought to another — are the mortar holding them together. Smooth transitions help readers move effortlessly from one thought to another.

Now put it all on paper

Turn your note-card draft into a written rough draft. Using your cards as your guide, sit down and write.

Double- or triple-space your draft, so that it will be easy to edit later on. After you are finished with a note card, put a check mark at the bottom of the card.

If you decide that you won't include information from a particular card, don't throw the card away...yet. Keep it in a separate stack. You may decide to fit in that piece of information in another part of your paper. Or you may change your mind after you read your rough draft and decide to include the information after all.

Help for when you get stuck

Got writer's block already? Here are a few tricks to get you unstuck.

✎ Pretend you're writing a letter to a good friend, and tell him or her everything you have learned about your subject and why you believe your thesis is correct.

✎ Use everyday language. Too many people get so hung up on using fancy words and phrases that they forget that their goal is communication. Simpler is better. Drop the dollar words and settle for the 25-centers.

✎ Type *some*thing. Once you have written that first sentence — even if it's really *bad* — your brain will start to generate spontaneous ideas.

✎ Don't edit yourself! As you write your rough draft, don't keep beating yourself up with negatives. Remember, your goal at this point is just a *rough* draft.

✎ Keep moving. If you get hung up on a particular section, don't sit there stewing over it for hours...or even many minutes. Just write a quick note about what you plan to cover in that section, and go on.

✎ If you can't get even that much out, skip the section altogether and come back to it later. Force yourself to make it all the way through your paper, with as few stops as possible.

Document your sources

To avoid plagiarism, you must document the source when you put any of the following in your paper:

✎ Quotations taken from a published source.

✎ Someone else's theories or ideas.

✎ Someone else's sentences, phrases, or special expressions.

✎ Facts, figures, and research data compiled by someone else.

✎ Graphs, pictures, and charts designed by someone else.

There are some exceptions. You don't need to document the source of a fact, theory, or expression that is common knowledge.

And you also do not need a source note when you use a phrase or expression for which there is no known author.

For a test of whether a statement needs a source note, ask yourself whether readers would otherwise think that you had come up with the information or idea all by yourself. If the answer is yes, you need a source note. If you're in doubt, include a source note anyway.

Footnotes

For many years, the preferred way to credit sources was the footnote. Two other forms of documentation, endnotes and parenthetical notes, are popular now as well.

A footnote is a source note that appears at the bottom of a page of text. You put a raised (superscript) number at the end of the statement or fact you need to document, which tells your readers to look at the bottom of the page for a note about the source of the data.

What goes in a footnote? The same information that's in the bibliography listing. *And* the exact page number the information appears on.

In front of that source note, you put the same superscript number as you put next to the statement or fact in your text.

There is no limit to the number of footnotes you may have in your paper. Number each footnote consecutively, starting with the number 1. For every footnote "flag" in your paper, be sure there is a corresponding source note at the bottom of the page.

Like bibliography listings, different authorities cite different rules for setting up footnotes. Ask your teacher whose rules you are to follow.

If your teacher doesn't have a preference, you might as well use the Modern Language Association of America (MLA) rules, which I use as well. Also, be sure to refer to **Improve Your Writing** for a more in-depth examination of source documentation.

(The MLA guidelines are used primarily for papers in the arts and humanities. If you are doing a paper for a physical or social science class, check with your teacher or professor as to which style you are to follow. Specific — and different — style sheets are used in biology, chemistry, math, physics, engineering, psychology, and so forth.)

Step 8: Do additional research

Did you discover any gaps in your research as you put together your first draft? Raise some questions that you need additional information to answer? If so, now's the time to head for the library for one last crack at the books.

Step 9: Write the second draft

The goal for this phase is to edit for meaning — improve the flow of your paper, organize your thoughts better, clarify confusing points, and strengthen weak arguments.

Focus on all of the problem areas you found. Add new data or information, if need be. Play with sentences, paragraphs, and even entire sections. If you're working with a computer, this is fairly easy to do. You can flip words, cut and add sentences, and rearrange whole pages with a few keystrokes.

As you review your rough draft, ask yourself the following questions:

- ✎ Do your thoughts move logically from one point to the next?

- ✎ Is the meaning of every sentence and paragraph crystal clear?

- ✎ Does every sentence make a point — or support one?

✎ Do you move smoothly from one paragraph to the next?

✎ Do you support your conclusions with solid evidence—research data, examples, statistics?

✎ Do you include a good *mix* of evidence—quotes from experts, scientific data, personal experiences, historical examples?

✎ Do you have a solid introduction and conclusion?

✎ Did you write in your own words and style, without merely stringing together phrases and quotes "borrowed" from other authors?

✎ Have you explained your subject thoroughly? (Don't assume that readers have more knowledge about it than they actually do. Remember: *You're* familiar with the topic now, but you've spent *weeks* on it. Just because something is now obvious to you doesn't mean your readers will know what you're talking about.)

✎ Have you convinced your readers that your thesis is valid?

✎ Is there information that, while correct and informative, just doesn't belong? Cut it out!

✎ Have you maintained a consistent point of view (i.e., first, second, or third person throughout)?

✎ Does your last paragraph successfully summarize the entire paper and effectively "close" your argument?

When you finish editing for content and meaning, print or type a clean copy of your paper, then double-check all of your facts for accuracy:

✎ Did you spell names, terms, and places correctly?

When you quoted dates and statistics, did you get your numbers straight?

 Do you have a source note (or preliminary source note) for every fact, expression or idea that is not your own?

 If you quoted material from a source, did you quote that source exactly, word for word, comma for comma, and did you put the material in quotation marks?

Mark any corrections on your new draft. Again, use a colored pen or pencil so you'll easily spot corrections later.

Now take an even closer look at your sentences and paragraphs. Try to make them smoother, tighter, easier to understand.

 Is there too much fat? Seize every opportunity to make the same point in fewer words.

 Are there places where phrasing or construction is awkward? Try to rearrange the sentence or section so that it has a better flow.

 Did you use descriptive, colorful words? Did you tell your reader "The planes were damaged" or paint a more colorful and creative picture: "The planes were broken-down hulks of rusted metal—bullet-ridden, neglected warbirds that could barely limp down the runway"?

 Consult a thesaurus for synonyms that work better than the words you originally chose.

 Have you overused particular words? Constantly using the same words makes your writing boring. Check a thesaurus for other possibilities.

 How do the words _sound_? When you read your paper aloud, does it flow like a rhythmic piece of music or plod along like a dirge? Vary the length of your sentences and paragraphs to make your writing more exciting.

✎ Always remember the point of the paper—to communicate your ideas as clearly and concisely as possible. So don't get lost in the details. Relax. If you have to choose between that "perfect" word and the most organized paper imaginable, opt for the latter.

Again, mark corrections on your draft with a colored pen or pencil. No need to retype your paper yet—unless it's gotten so marked up that it's hard to read.

Step 10: Check spelling and grammar

All right, here's the part that almost nobody enjoys: It's time to rid your paper of any mistakes in grammar and spelling.

I've told you your thoughts are the most important element of your paper. It's true. But it's also true that glaring mistakes in grammar and spelling will lead your teacher to believe that you are either careless or downright ignorant—neither of which will bode well for your final grade.

So get out your dictionary and a reference book on English usage and grammar. Scour your paper, sentence by sentence, marking corrections with your colored pen or pencil. Look for:

✎ **Misspelled words.** Check every word. If you're using a spell-checking computer program, be careful of sound-alike words. "There" might be spelled correctly, but not if you meant to write "their."

✎ **Incorrect punctuation.** Review the rules for placement of commas, quotation marks, periods, and other punctuation. Make sure you follow those rules throughout your paper.

 Incorrect sentence structure. Look for dangling participles, split infinitives, sentences that end in prepositions, and other various grammar no-no's.

Step 11: Have someone *else* proofread

Retype your paper, making all those corrections you marked during the last step. Format the paper according to the teacher's instructions. Incorporate your final footnotes and bibliography.

Give your paper a title, one that's as short and sweet as possible, but tells readers what they can expect to learn from your paper.

Find someone who is a good proofreader — a parent, relative, friend — and ask him or her to proofread your paper before you put together the final draft.

Steps 12, 13, and 14: The final draft

Incorporate any changes or errors your proofreader may have caught. Type the final draft. Proof it again — very carefully.

Here are a couple of tricks of the trade: 1) **Read your paper aloud**. Go ahead — shout it from the rooftops! It's amazing how easily you'll discover misplaced words, poor grammar, even a misspelling or two. 2) **Read your paper backwards**. This forces you to focus on each individual word and is a sensational way to pick up misspellings.

When everything's absolutely perfect, head right for the copy shop. Pay the buck or two it costs to make a copy of your paper. After all your hard work, you want to be sure you have a backup copy in case you lose or damage your original.

Last step? Put your paper in a new manuscript binder or folder. Then, turn it in — on time, of course!

'Twas the night before the deadline...

Despite my best advice, some of you will undoubtedly choose to delay working on your paper until the last possible instant. Many of you may well suffer from the same feelings of malaise and procrastination that infected much of my dorm when papers were due. A lot of my friends seemed hell-bent on finding something, *anything*, that could be done instead of actually sitting down and writing that flaming paper.

I received this exaggerated but all-too-familiar "paper writing plan" via e-mail from a colleague's fraternity. Does it sound like your systematic approach? Do you believe it's a valid way to proceed? Have I been writing all this for nothing?

How to Write a Paper

1. Sit in a straight, comfortable chair in a well-lit place with plenty of freshly sharpened pencils.

2. Carefully read over the assignment. Underline or highlight key instructions.

3. Walk down to the vending machines and buy some coffee so you can concentrate.

4. On the way back to your room, stop and visit with your friend from class. If he hasn't started *his* paper either, walk to McDonald's and buy a hamburger to help you concentrate. If, instead, he proudly shows off his paper — typed,

double-spaced, and bound in one of those irritating see-thru plastic folders—hurt him.

5. When you get back to your room, sit in a straight, comfortable chair in a clean well-lit place with plenty of freshly sharpened pencils.

6. Read over the assignment again to make absolutely certain you understand it. Highlight it in a different color.

7. You know, you haven't written to that kid you met at camp since fourth grade—better write that letter now and get it out of the way so you can concentrate.

8. Inspect your teeth in the bathroom mirror. Floss. Twice.

9. Listen to one song on your favorite CD. And that's it. I mean it. As soon as it's over start writing that paper.

10. Listen to the rest of the CD.

11. Rearrange all your CDs into alphabetical order.

12. Phone your friend to see if *he*'s started writing yet. Exchange derogatory remarks about your teacher, the course, the university, and the world at large.

13. Sit in a straight, comfortable chair in a clean, well-lit place with plenty of freshly sharpened pencils.

14. Read over the assignment again; roll the words across your tongue; savor their special flavor. Choose at least three more highlighter colors.

15. Check the newspaper listings to make sure you aren't missing something truly worthwhile on TV. **NOTE:** When you have a paper due in less than 12 hours, anything on TV—from *Masterpiece Theater* to *Rocky & Bullwinkle*—is truly

worthwhile, with only two exceptions: a) Any show involving bowling; and b) any Suzanne Sommers' infomercial.

16. Look at your tongue in the bathroom mirror.

17. Sit down and do some serious thinking about your plans for the future.

18. Open your door; check to see if there are any mysterious, trench-coated strangers lurking in the hall.

19. Sit in a straight, comfortable chair in a clean, well-lit place with plenty of freshly sharpened pencils.

20. Read over the assignment one more time, just for the heck of it.

21. Scoot your chair across the room to the window and watch the sunrise.

22. Lie face down on the floor. Moan and thrash about.

23. Leap up and write that paper as fast as you can type!

Presuming you have no choice but to be late, for reasons good or bad, you might want to find a copy of my book *Last Minute Study Tips* to figure out how to write a good paper when there's little or no time to spare!

Oral reports

There are some key differences between writing a report and presenting it orally, especially if you don't want to make the mistake of just reading your report in front of the class.

If you've been assigned to give a talk for a class, it will probably fall into one of the following categories:

 Exposition: a straightforward statement of facts.

 Argument: trying to change the opinions of at least a portion of the audience.

 Description: providing a visual picture to your listeners.

 Narration: storytelling.

The most common forms of oral reports assigned in school will be exposition and argument. You'll find that you will research and organize information for these types of speeches pretty much the way you would a term paper.

As you gather information for your report, making notes on index cards as you did for your term paper, keep this in mind: In order for you to be effective, you must use some different techniques when you *tell* your story rather than *write* it. Here are a few:

 Don't make your topic too broad. This advice, offered for preparing written reports as well, is even more important when preparing a talk. Try giving an effective speech on Eleanor Roosevelt, Jane Austen's novels, or the U.S. military in 15 minutes—frequently the amount of time assigned for oral reports. These topics are more suited to a series of books!

Eleanor Roosevelt's part in changing the role of the First Lady, the way the movie "Clueless" failed to meet the standards set by Austen's *Emma*, or the pros and cons of inoculating all U.S. military personnel with the anthrax vaccine are more manageable. Narrowing the scope of your talk will help you research and organize it more effectively.

✎ **Don't overuse statistics.** While they're very important for lending credibility, too many will weigh down your speech and bore your audience.

✎ **Anecdotes add color and life to your talk.** But use them sparingly, because they can slow down your speech. Get to the punch line before the yawns start.

✎ **Be careful with quotes.** Unlike a term paper, a speech allows you to establish yourself as an authority with less fear of being accused of plagiarism. So you can present a lot more facts without attribution. (But you'd better have the sources in case you're asked about your facts.)

I've found that trying to shuffle a bunch of papers in front of a class is difficult and that note cards that fit in the palm of your hand are a lot easier to use. But only if the notes on them are very short and to the point, to act as "triggers" rather than verbatim cue cards—hanging on to 300 note cards is as difficult as a sheaf of papers.

Remember: You'll actually be holding these cards in your sweaty palms and speaking from them, so write *notes,* not whole sentences. The shorter the notes—and the more often you practice your report so each note triggers the right information—the more effective your report will be. (And the less you will have to look at them, making eye contact with your class and teacher easier.)

Here are ways to make oral reports more effective:

✎ Pick out one person to talk to—preferably a friend, but an animated and/or interested person will do—and direct your talk to them.

✎ *Practice, practice, practice* your presentation. Jangled nerves are often the result of a lack of confidence. The better you know your material, the less nervous you'll be and the better and more spontaneous your presentation.

✎ If you suffer from involuntary "shakes" at the mere thought of standing in front of a roomful of people, make sure you can use a lectern, desk, or something to cling to.

✎ Take a deep breath before you go to the front of the class. And don't worry about pausing, even taking another deep breath or two, if you lose your place or find your confidence slipping away.

✎ If every trick in the world still doesn't steady your nerves, consider taking a public speaking course (Dale Carnegie, *et al*), joining the Toastmasters Club, or seeking out similar extracurricular help.

CHAPTER 8

How to "Ace" Any Test

Q UIZZES. MIDTERMS. FINALS. PSAT. ACT. SAT. GMAT. GRE. LSAT. Civil Service exams. Aptitude tests. Employment tests.

Throughout your educational life — and, more than likely, the *rest* of your life — testing will be an inevitable if sometimes frightening and distressing reality. The sooner you learn the techniques of preparing for, taking, and mastering tests, the better off you'll be.

What do they want to know?

Many tests are as much a measure of the *way* you study — your ability to organize a mountain of material — as they are a measure of your knowledge of the material itself. This is especially true of any test that purports to measure knowledge spread across the years and your mastery of such a broad spectrum of material—the SAT; GRE; bar or medical exam; exams for nurses, CPAs, financial planners; or the three days of oral exams my alma mater put everyone through. Which means the better you _study_, the better your _score_ will probably be on such tests.

There are, as we've already seen, ways to organize your studying to achieve maximum results in minimal time. There are a great number of such techniques to use when studying for tests of any kind.

Before you can decide how to study for a particular test, it's imperative that you know exactly what you're being tested _on_. Preparing for a weekly quiz is far different than preparing for a final exam. And the biggest final of your life is child's play compared to "monster tests" like the oral exams I faced before they allowed me to graduate college—which covered everything I was supposed to have learned in four years.

Studying for a standardized test like the PSAT, SAT, ACT, or GRE is also completely different—you can't pull out your textbook and, knowing what chapters are being included, just "bone up."

The structure of the test is also of paramount importance, not necessarily in terms of how you study, but how you tackle it once you get your test book.

What are you afraid of?

Tests are scary creatures. So before I start doling out test-taking techniques, let's tackle one of the key problems many of you will face—test anxiety, that all-too-common reaction to tests characterized by sweaty palms, a blank mind, and the urge to flee to Pago Pago on the next available cargo ship.

What does it mean when someone proclaims she doesn't "test well"? It may mean she doesn't *study* well (or, at the very least, *prepare* well). Or it could mean she is easily distracted, unprepared for the type of test she is confronting, or simply unprepared mentally to take *any* test (which may include mentally sabotaging herself into a poor score or grade, even though she knows the material backwards and forwards).

Take heart—very few people look forward to a test; more of you are afraid of tests than you'd think. But that doesn't mean you *have* to fear them.

Since we all recognize the competitive nature of tests, being in the right frame of mind when taking them is important. Some of us rise to the occasion when facing such a challenge. Others are thrown off balance by the pressure. Both reactions probably have little to do with one's level of knowledge, relative intelligence, or preparation. The smartest kids in your class may be the ones most afraid of tests.

Generally speaking, the best way to avoid the pitfalls of the extraordinary pressures of a testing situation is to place yourself in that environment as often as possible. Yep. Practice helps. Get permission from your teachers to retake some old tests to practice the test-taking techniques and exorcise the High Anxiety Demon. Take a couple of standardized tests that your counseling office might have, too, since the fill-in-the-box answer sheets and questions in printed form have their own set of rules.

There are also some surprisingly simple steps you can take to give yourself an edge by being less *on* edge.

Dealing with test anxiety

Few people enter a testing site cool, calm, and ready for action. Most of us have various butterflies gamboling in our stomachs, sweat glands operating in overdrive, and a sincere desire to be somewhere else...*anywhere* else.

Even if you're just entering high school, you have a few years of tests under your belt and should have some idea of how well or poorly you react to a testing situation. If the answer is "not well," start trying some of the following options until you find the one(s) that work for you.

"I know I can, I know I can"

The more pressure you put on yourself — the larger you allow a test (and, of course, your hoped-for good scores) to loom in your own mind — the less you are helping yourself. (And the bigger the test really *is,* the more likely you are to keep reminding yourself of its importance.)

No matter how important a test really may be to your career — and, let's face it, your scores on some *can* have a major effect on where you go to college, whether you go to graduate school, whether you get the job you want — it is just as important to *de-emphasize* that test's importance in your mind. This should have no effect on your preparation — you should still study as if your life depended on a superior score. It might!

A friend of mine signed up not long ago to take the Law School Admission Test (LSAT), not just once, but twice. The first time, he did okay, but not great. By the time the second date rolled around, he had come to his senses and decided not to become a lawyer. But since he had already paid for the thing, he took the LSAT again anyway. Are you already ahead of me? That's right — a 15-percent improvement with *no* studying.

Keeping the whole experience in perspective might also help: Twenty years from now, nobody will remember, or care, what you scored on *any* test — no matter how life-determining you feel that test is right now.

Of course, you *can* make it easier to do all this by *not* going out of your way — certainly before an especially big or important test — to add *more* stress to an already stressful life. Two days before the SAT is *not* the time to dump a boy-friend, move, change jobs, take out a big loan, or create any other waves in your normally placid river of life.

Watch out for those "friends" who call you the night before the exam with, "I just found out we have to know Chapter 12!" Don't fall into their trap. Instead of dialing 911, calmly remind them that the printed sheet the professor passed out two weeks ago clearly says that the test will cover chapters 6 through 11. Then hang up, get on with your life, and let them wring their hands all the way to the bottom of the grading sheet. (Of course, if *you* don't bother to check what's going to be on the test, a call like this *will* panic you...and waste your time.)

How to lower your AQ (Anxiety Quotient)

To come to terms with the "importance" of a test, read the list below. Knowing the answers to as many of these questions as possible will help reduce your anxiety.

1. What material will the exam cover?
2. How many total points are possible?
3. What percentage of my semester grade is based on this exam?
4. How much time will I have to take the exam?
5. Where will the exam be held?
6. What kinds of questions will be on the exam (matching, multiple choice, essay, true/false)?
7. How many points will be assigned to each question? Will certain types of questions count more than others? How many of each type of question will be on the exam?
8. Will it be an open-book exam?
9. What can I take in with me? Calculator? Candy bar? Other material crucial to my success?
10. Will I be penalized for wrong answers?

Hit the road, Jack

You've already found that scheduling breaks during your study routine makes it easier for you to focus on your books and complete your assignments faster and with more concentration. Scheduling breaks during tests has the same effect.

No matter what the time limits or pressures, don't feel you cannot afford such a brief respite. You may need it _most_ when you're convinced you can _least_ afford it, just as those who most need time-management techniques "just don't have the time" to learn them.

I'm relaxing as fast as I can!

If your mind is a jumble of facts and figures, names and dates, you may find it difficult to zero in on the specific details you need to recall, even if you know all the material backwards and forwards. The adrenaline rushing through your system may just make "instant retrieval" impossible.

The simplest relaxation technique is deep breathing. Lean back in your chair, relax your muscles, and take three very deep breaths (count to 10 while you hold each one).

There are a variety of meditation techniques that may also work for you. Each is based on a similar principle—focusing your mind on one thing to the exclusion of everything else. While you're concentrating on the object of your meditation (even if the object is nothing, a nonsense word, or a spot on the wall), your mind can't be thinking about anything else, which allows it to slow down a bit.

The next time you can't focus, try sitting back, taking three deep breaths, and concentrating for a minute or two on the word "Mu." When you're done, you should be in a far more relaxed state and ready to tackle any test.

If you feel you need such help, consider learning some sort of meditation technique or even self-hypnosis.

Preparing for great test scores

Some rites of preparation are pertinent to any test, from a weekly quiz to the SAT and everything in between:

Plan ahead

I admit it. When I was a student, even in college, my attention span tended to be bounded by weekends. Tell me in October that there'd be a big test the first week of December and I'd remember, probably, around November 30th.

Of such habits are cramming, crib sheets, and failing marks made.

The key to avoiding all of these unpleasantries is *regular, periodic review*. The more often you review, the less often you will have to pull all-nighters the week of the test. You already will have stayed on top of the material, written down and asked questions that arose from your reviews, and gone over class and textbook notes to make sure you understand everything. Your last-minute review will be relatively leisurely and organized, not feverish and harried.

Use *two* alarm clocks

Doing poorly on a test is discouraging. Doing poorly on a test you felt ready for is depressing. Missing the test entirely is devastating. It's imperative that you know when and where all tests are scheduled and allow ample time to get to them.

If you're still in high school, getting to a particular test shouldn't be too hard—it will probably be held during your regular class period, in your normal classroom.

But in college, tests may be scheduled at hours different than the normal class period...and at entirely different sites.

Likewise, major out-of-school tests like the PSAT and SAT may not even be held at your school. In such cases, make sure you allow enough time to drive to, or be driven to, wherever you have to be — especially if you're not quite sure how to get there!

As soon as you know the time and location of any major test, enter it on your weekly calendar. Whether in high school, college, or grad school, most schools set aside a week, two, or even more for final exams. This exam period is usually clearly marked in your college handbook, announced in class (usually on the first day), and printed on your class syllabus.

Make optional assignments mandatory

Sometimes, in addition to your regular reading and other assignments, the teacher will assign optional reading at the beginning of a course. These books, articles, and so forth, may never be discussed in any class — but material from them may be included on a test, especially a final exam. If you have neglected to add this supplementary reading to your regular weekly assignments calendar, but wish to read it before the test, make sure you allow enough time to buy or find these books. A lot of other students may have also left such reading to the last minute, and you may be unable to find the material you need if you wait too long.

Pens, pencils...a candy bar

Lastly, bring whatever materials you need to the test, from pens and pencils to calculators. I also recommend — especially for a long test like the SAT or ACT — that you bring along a candy bar, hard candies, a granola bar, or some other "quick energy" snack to help wake you up when you need to give yourself a figurative slap in the face.

Although many testing booklets will include room for notes, it may not be sufficient for your purposes. If you are asked to write three, five, or even more essay questions, you will want a lot of scratch paper to outline and organize your thoughts before you put pen to paper. Likewise, a particularly complex math test may quickly use up every square inch of margin. So bring along a separate writing tablet or even a stack of scrap paper. There are few situations in which their use won't be allowed.

If you didn't listen before...

Review, review, review. If you don't follow my advice for periodic review, you must be sure, especially for midterms and finals, to set aside the time to do the review and studying you need in the week or two before the test. Most colleges — and many high schools — offer a reading or study period, usually the week before midterms or finals, where no classes are offered. Library hours are often extended. Take advantage of this time.

The more material you need to review, the more important it is to clear your schedule. A four-, five-, or six-course load covering 20, 40, or more books, lectures and discussions, papers, and projects, easily generates hundreds of pages of notes. Reviewing, understanding, and studying them will require your full-time effort for a week, even two. So make sure all other end-of-term work, especially major projects like papers, are out of the way.

Whether you need to schedule a solid two weeks for a complete review or just two or three days because you have already reviewed most of your course work on a regular basis, make sure you schedule the time you've allocated on your weekly calendar, allowing more time for the subjects in which you are weakest, of course.

Why cramming doesn't work

We've all done it at one time or another, with one excuse or another — waited until the last minute and then tried to cram a week's or month's or entire semester's worth of work into a single night or weekend. Did it work for you? I doubt it.

The reality is that cramming works—on one level—for a small minority of students. Somehow, they're able to shove more "stuff" into short-term memory than the rest of us and actually remember it, at least for 24 hours. After those 24 hours? Gone with the wind. Which means if they managed to do well on a weekly quiz, all that cramming didn't do them a bit of good for the upcoming midterm or final. And it certainly didn't manage to affect at all what they actually learned from the course, or what they can carry with them in understanding and knowledge long after the course is just a memory.

The rest of us don't even get that smidgen of good news—after a night of no sleep and too much coffee, we're lucky if we remember where the test _is_ the next morning. A couple of hours later, trying to stay awake long enough to make it back to bed, we not only haven't learned anything, we haven't even done very well on the test we crammed for!

That's probably the best reason of all not to cram—it just doesn't work!

How to cram anyway

Nevertheless, despite your resolve, best intentions, and firm conviction that cramming is a losing proposition, you may well find yourself—though hopefully not too often—in the position of needing to do something the night before a test you haven't studied for at all. If so, there are some rules to follow that will make your night of cramming at least marginally successful:

Be realistic about what you can do. You absolutely _cannot_ master an entire semester's worth of work in a single night, especially if your class attendance has been sporadic (or non-existent) and you've skimmed two books out of a syllabus of two dozen. The _more_ information you try to cram in, the _less_ effective you will be.

Needless to say, being realistic means a sober assessment of your situation—you're hanging by your thumbs and are just trying to avoid that fall into the boiling oil. Avoiding the oil, saving the damsel in distress, and inheriting the kingdom ("acing" the test) is a bit too much to ask for, no matter whom your Fairy Godmother. And, of course, you are *not* expecting to remember anything about the course one day after the test, are you?

Be selective and study in depth. The more you've managed to miss, the more selective you need to be in organizing your cram session. You *can't* study it all. Use every technique in this chapter to separate the wheat from the chaff, (or, at least, the ones you expect to be on the test from the ones you don't). Then study the topics one by one, only moving to the second when you feel you have an excellent grasp of the first. It's better in this case to know a lot about a little rather than a little about a lot. You may get lucky and pick the three topics the three essays cover!

Massage your memory. Use every memory technique you know (and the ones in *Improve Your Memory* that you probably don't know) to maximize what you're able to retain in your short-term memory. Repetition is key; reciting out loud is a good idea.

Know when to give up. When you can't remember your name, give up and get some sleep. Better to arrive at the exam with some sleep under your belt and feeling as relaxed as possible.

Consider an early morning rather than a late-night cram. Especially if you're a "morning" person, but even if you're not, I've personally found it more effective to go to bed early and get up early rather than go to bed late and get up exhausted. Such a plan also requires that you remember all this stuff for less time.

Spend the first few minutes writing down whatever you remember now but are afraid you'll forget. A suggestion good at any time but especially when your mind is trying to hold onto so many facts and figures it seems ready to explode.

Get a copy of my book—*Last Minute Study Tips*. It will help you prepare for a test that's weeks, days, hours, or just minutes away...and do better on it.

When in doubt, ask

Yes, there are teachers who test you on the most mundane details of their course, requiring you to review every book, every note, every scribble.

I don't think most teachers work that way. You will more than likely be tested on some subset of the course, those particular topics or problems or facts or figures the teacher believes most important.

How do you know what those are? To put it bluntly, how do you know what's going to be on the test? An important question, especially since I keep urging you to tailor and organize your studying based on such information.

Teachers give many clues. In general, the more often you see or hear the same material, the more important it probably is and the more likely it will show up on a test. Consider a subhead in your textbook repeated twice in the same lecture and repeated again just a week before the test, a megaphone announcing, "This is on the test!"

A fact or topic need not be repeated in order to scream "Learn me!" Just as you learned to watch a teacher's body language and listen for verbal clues to identify noteworthy topics, you'll learn to identify topics the teacher indicates—nonverbally—are the most important. Your teacher's attitude *toward* note-taking may well tip you off, as well. If he or she requires you to take detailed notes—even wants them turned in (sometimes in high school, rarely in college)—I'd figure that your class notes are far and away more important than the textbook(s).

Have you saved earlier tests and quizzes from that class? Returned exams, especially if they contain a lot of comments from your teacher, should give you an excellent indication of where to concentrate your study time.

Is it wrong to ask the teacher what kind of test to expect? Absolutely not. Will he or she always tell you? Absolutely not. But it is not wrong to research that teacher's tests from previous years—students a year or two ahead of you can sometimes be of invaluable help in this effort.

Why? Like most of us, teachers are creatures of habit. While you certainly shouldn't expect to find questions that will be duplicated, you can glean a few key things from previous tests, like the format the teacher seems to prefer and the areas that seem to be stressed. Don't take any of this as a "given," however. Even creatures of the most set habits can turn over a new leaf now and then.

More list-making, please

Once you've discovered the type of test facing you, you want to figure out what's actually going to be *on* it (and, hence, what you actually need to study). Remember: It's rarely, if ever, "everything."

In general, take the time to eliminate from consideration, with the possible exception of a cursory review, material you are convinced is simply not important enough to be included on an upcoming test. This will automatically give you more time to concentrate on those areas you are sure *will* be included.

Then create a "To Study" sheet for each test. On it, list specific books to review, notes to recheck, specific topics and concepts to go over. Then check off each item as you study it. This is akin to breaking the paper-writing process into 14 smaller, easier-to-accomplish steps and will have the same effect—to minimize procrastination, logically organize your studying, and give you ongoing "jolts" of accomplishment as you complete each item.

Test yourself

Just as you have made it a habit to write down questions as you study your texts, why not try to construct your own tests? The harder you make them, the better prepared and more confident you will be walking into the test.

Practice tests offer some real advantages, whether you're studying for a weekly quiz, the SAT, or your bar exam. In fact, the longer and more "standardized" the test, the more important it is to be familiar with its structure, its rules, and its traps.

First and foremost, familiarization with whatever type of test you're taking is vitally important, as it enables you to strategically study the material (prioritize) and strategically attack the test (organize). Familiarization breeds comfort and, as I've pointed out more than once, being comfortable — *relaxed* — is a key component to doing well.

Familiarization also breeds organization, allowing you to concentrate on the test itself and not on its structure. This gives you more time to actually *take* the test rather than figure it out. It also reduces the effect of whatever time restraints the test imposes on you. The greater the time restraints, the more practicing will enable you to deal with them on the actual test, minimizing the pressure.

Last but not least, taking practice tests is a highly effective way to study and remember the material.

Test-day rules and reminders

If the test is not simply during a regular class period, make sure to arrive at the test site early. Based on your preferences (from Chapter 2), sit where you like.

Be careful, however. There may be some variations you have to take into account. In a test where there are 200 or 300 people in a room, there is a distinct advantage to sitting up front: You can hear the instructions and the answers to questions better, and you generally get the test first.

Go all the way

Begin at the beginning. Then move through to the end. No, I'm not talking about taking the exam, I'm talking about looking through the booklet or taking a glance at all the questions. If you have permission to go all the way through it, do that before you even start testing. Give yourself an overview of what lies ahead. That way you can spot the easier sections (and do them first) and get an idea of the point values assigned to each section.

Know the ground rules

Will you be penalized for guessing? The teacher, for example, may inform you that you will earn two points for every correct answer but *lose* one point for every incorrect one. This will certainly affect whether you guess or skip the question—or, at the very least, how many potential answers you feel you need to eliminate before the odds of guessing are in your favor.

In the case of a standardized test like the SAT, ACT, or GRE, read the instructions on a previous test before you go to the test site. (There are numerous books that include "actual tests" in their prep books.) Then just skim the instructions in your booklet or on the computer to make sure nothing has changed. It will save you minutes—time that is precious indeed during any such test.

Are the questions or sections weighted? Some tests may have two, three, or more sections, some of which count for very little (10 or 20 percent of your final score) while one, usually a major essay, may be more heavily weighted (50 percent or more of your grade). This should drastically alter the amount of time you spend on each section.

Discriminate and eliminate

There is usually nothing wrong with guessing, unless, of course, you know wrong answers will be penalized. Even then, as I've pointed out, guessing is not necessarily wrong. The question is how *much* to guess.

If there is no penalty for wrong answers, *never* leave an answer blank. (As far as the SAT is concerned, there really isn't a penalty for guessing, so don't leave any answer blank!) But you should also do everything you can to increase your odds of getting it right. If every multiple-choice question gives you four possible answers, you have a 25-percent chance of being right (and thus a 75-percent chance of being wrong) each time you have to guess.

But if you can eliminate a single answer—one you are reasonably certain cannot be right—your chances of being correct increase to 33 percent.

If you can get down to a choice between two answers, it's just like flipping a coin: 50-50. In the long run, you will guess as many right as wrong. Even if there is a penalty for guessing, I'd probably pick an answer if I'd managed to increase my chances of getting the right one to 50-50.

Presuming you've managed to eliminate one or more answers but are still unsure of the correct answer and have no particular way to eliminate further, here are some real insider tips to make your guess more "educated":

- ✎ If two answers sound alike, choose neither.

- ✎ The most "obvious" answer to a difficult question is probably wrong, but an answer that is close to it is probably right.

- ✎ If the answers that are left to a mathematical question cover a broad range, choose the number in the middle.

- ✎ If two quantities are very close, choose one of them.

✎ If two numbers differ only by a decimal point (and the others aren't close), choose one of them. (Example: 2.3, 40, 1.5, 6, 15; I'd go with 1.5 or 15. If I could at least figure out from the question where the decimal point should go, even better!)

✎ If two answers to a math problem *look* alike—either formulas or shapes—choose one of them.

Remember: This is not the way to "ace" a test—these are just some tried-and-true ways to increase your guessing power when *you have absolutely nothing else to go on and nothing left to do.*

Should you go back, recheck your work, and change a guess? How valid was that first guess? Surprisingly, perhaps, statistics show it was probably pretty darned good (presuming you had some basis for guessing in the first place). So good that you should only change it if:

✎ It really was just a wild guess and, upon further thought, you conclude that answer really should be eliminated (in which case your next guess is, at least, not quite so wild).

✎ You remembered something that changes the odds of your guess completely. (Even better, the answer to a later question helped you figure out the answer to this one!)

✎ You miscalculated on a math problem.

✎ You misread the question (didn't notice a "not," a "never," an "always," or some other important qualifier).

What if you eliminate four of the five answers and are convinced that the one that's left—your supposedly "right" answer—is flat-out wrong? Eliminate *it* and start your analysis all over again with the other four potential answers (one of which, you are now declaring, is the right one!).

Guess and guess again?

If you do guess at any of the objective questions and you are getting your test paper returned to you, place a little dot or other symbol beside them. That way you will know how successful your guessing was.

When you think you have finished a whole section, double-check to see if that's true. Look on the answer sheet or in the blue book to make sure all the questions have been answered.

It's a long race—pace yourself

If you have 100 multiple-choice questions and you have 50 minutes allotted for that section, you don't have to be MIT material to figure that you should spend a maximum of 30 seconds on each answer.

Don't depend on a wall clock to tell you the time. Bring your watch.

Answer every fourth question

Read and understand the directions. As I stressed earlier, you could seemingly do everything _right_, but not follow your teacher's explicit directions, in which case everything's _wrong._

If you're supposed to check off _every_ correct answer to each question in a multiple-choice test—and you're assuming only _one_ answer to each question is correct—you're going to miss a lot of answers!

If you're to pick one essay question out of three, or two out of five, that's a lot different than trying to answer every one. You won't do it. And even if you do, the teacher will probably only grade the first two. Because you needed to allocate enough time to do the other three, it's highly doubtful your first two answers will be so detailed and perfect that they will be able to stand alone.

And be aware of time. Again, if questions or sections are weighted, you will want to make sure you allow extra time for those that count the most. Better to do a superior job on the two sections that count for 90 percent of the score and whip through the 10-percent section as the teacher is collecting test booklets.

If there are pertinent facts or formulas you're afraid you'll forget, write them down somewhere in your test booklet before you do anything else. It won't take much time and it could save you some serious memory jogs later.

First out could be first failed

Leave time at the end to recheck your answers.

Speaking of time, don't make a habit of leaving tests early. There is little to be gained from supposedly impressing the teacher and other students with how smart you (think you) are by being first to finish. Take the time to make sure you've done your best. If you are completely satisfied with your answers to all of the questions, it's fine to leave, even if you are first. But in general, slowing down will help you avoid careless mistakes.

Likewise, don't worry about what everybody else is doing. Even if you're the last person left, who cares? Everybody else could have failed, no matter how early and confidently they strode from the room! So take all the time you need and do the best you can.

16 tips for "acing" multiple-choice tests

1. Be careful you don't read too much into questions. Don't try to second-guess the test preparer, get too elaborate, and ruin the answer.
2. Underline the key words.
3. If two choices are very similar, the answer is probably not either one of them.

4. If two choices are opposite, one of them is probably correct.

5. Don't go against your first impulse unless you are *sure* you were wrong.

6. Check for negatives and other words that are there to throw you off.

7. The answer is usually wrong if it contains "all," "always," "never," or "none." I repeat, usually.

8. The answer has a great chance of being right if it has "sometimes," "probably," or "some."

9. When you don't know the right answer, look for the wrong ones.

10. Don't eliminate an answer unless you actually know what every word means.

11. Read every answer (unless you are wildly guessing at the last minute and there's no penalty). Test makers have been known to place a "decoy" answer first—one that's oh-so-close to the right one—just to tempt you to pick it without even reading the other choices. Don't fall into their evil trap.

12. If it's a standardized test, consider transferring all the answers from one section to the answer sheet at the same time.

13. If you're supposed to read a long passage and then answer questions about it, read the questions *first*. That will tell you what you're looking for and *affect the way you read the passage*. If you are convinced you know the answer to a question before you even read the passage—and your answer is actually supplied—check it off and move right on.

14. The longest and/or most complicated answer to a question is often correct.

15. Be suspicious of choices that seem obvious to a 2-year-old. Why would the teacher give you such a gimme?

16. Likewise, don't give up on a question that, after one reading, seems hopelessly confusing or hard. Looking at it from a different angle, restating it in your own words, drawing a picture, whatever, may help you realize it's not as hard as you first thought.

Test-taking strategies

In addition to some of the general ideas we've talked about, there are very specific strategies to use depending on the type of test you're taking. Let's look at them one at a time.

All of the above again?

There are three ways to attack a multiple-choice test:

1. Start at the first question and keep going, question by question, until you reach the end, never leaving a question until you have either answered it fully or made an educated guess.

2. Answer every *easy* question—the ones you know the answers to without any thinking at all or those requiring the simplest calculations—first, then go back and do the harder ones.

3. Answer the *hardest* questions first, then go back and do the easy ones.

None of these three options is inherently right or wrong. Each may work for different individuals. (And I'm assuming that these three approaches are all in the context of the test format. Weighted sections may well affect your strategy.)

The first approach is, in one sense, the quickest, in that no time is wasted reading through the whole test trying to pick out either the easiest or hardest questions. Presuming you do not allow yourself to get stumped by a single question so that you spend an inordinate amount of time on it, it is probably the method most of you employ.

The second approach ensures that you will maximize your right answers—you're putting those you are certain of down first. It may also, presuming that you knock off these easy ones relatively fast, give you the most time to work on those that you find particularly vexing.

Many experts recommend this method because they maintain that answering so many questions one after another gives you immediate confidence to tackle the questions you're not sure about. If you find that you agree, then by all means use this strategy. However, you may consider just *noting* easy ones as you preread the test. This takes less time and, to me, delivers the same "confidence boost."

The last approach is actually the one I used. In fact, I made it a point to do the very hardest questions first, then work my way "down" the difficulty ladder. (Which means I often worked *backwards* since many test makers and teachers make their tests progressively more difficult.)

It may sound strange to you, so let me explain the psychology. I figured if time pressure starts getting to me at the end of the test, I would rather be in a position to answer the easiest questions—and a lot of them—in the limited time left, rather than ones I really had to think about. After all, by the end of the test, my mind was simply not working as well as it was at the beginning!

That's the major benefit of the third approach: When I was most "up," most awake, most alert, I tackled questions that required the most analysis, thinking, and interpretation. When I was most tired—near the end—I was answering the questions that were virtually "gimmes."

At the same time, I was also giving myself a *real* shot of confidence. As soon as I finished the first hard question, I already felt better. When I finished all of the hard ones, everything was downhill.

I would always, however, try to ensure adequate time to at least put down an answer for every question. Better to get one question wrong and complete three other answers than get one right and leave three blank. It is not the approach for everybody, but it may be right for you.

Don't fall into the "answer daze," that blank stare some students get when they can't think of an answer—for 10 minutes. Do *something*. Better to move on and get that one question wrong than waste invaluable time doing nothing.

50/50 odds aren't bad. True or false?

What can you do to increase your scores on true-false tests?

First of all, be more inclined to guess if you have to. After all, I encouraged you to guess on a multiple-choice test if you could eliminate enough wrong answers to get down to two, one of which is correct. Well, you're already there! So unless you are being penalized for guessing, guess away! (Even if you are being penalized, you may well want to take a shot if you have the faintest clue of the correct answer.)

What tricks do test makers incorporate in true-false tests? Here are three to watch out for:

Two parts (statements) that *are* true (or, at least, *may* be true) linked in such a way that the *whole* statement becomes false. Example: "Since many birds can fly, they use stones to grind their food." Many birds *do* fly, and birds *do* swallow stones to grind their food, but a *causal relationship* (the word "since") between the two clauses makes the whole statement false.

On a multiple-choice test, the longest and/or most complicated answer to a question is often correct—the test maker has been forced to add qualifying clauses or phrases to make that answer complete and unequivocal. The exact *opposite* is true regarding true-false tests: The longer and/or more complicated a statement in a true-false test, the *less* likely it's true since *every clause* of it must be true (and there are so many chances for a single part to be false).

Few broad, general statements are true *without exception.* Always be on your guard when you see the words "all," "always," "no," "never," or other absolutes. As long as you can think of a *single* example that proves such a statement false, then it is false. Be wary: There are statements with such absolutes that *are* true; they're just rare.

Mastering multiple-choice math

Process of elimination is important in finding the answers. There are some numbers to consider, also. For example, scan the following problem and see if you can figure out the answer without actually doing the math.

334 x 412 =

(A) 54,559

(B) 137,608

(C) 22,528

(D) 229,766

By performing one simple task, you can eliminate two of the possible answers. Multiply the last digits in each number (2 x 4). The answer must end in 8. So (A) and (D) have been eliminated...that fast!

Now, eyeball (B) and (C). Can you find the right answer quickly? Here you are doing educated guessing, known in math circles as "guesstimating." Look: 334 x 100 is 33,400. You should be able to do that without any tools. Therefore, (C) has to be wrong. You are left with (B).

Should you do the actual math to double-check your answer? I wouldn't. You are certain that (A) and (D) are wrong. Absolutely. You know that (C) is much too low. Mark (B) as the answer and move on.

Here are other ways to better your score on math tests:

✎ Try to figure out what is being asked, what principles are involved, what information is important, and what's not. Don't let extraneous data throw you off track. Make sure you know the *kind* of answer you're seeking: Is it a speed, weight, angle, exponent, square root?

✎ Whenever you can, "translate" formulas and numbers into words. Estimate the answer before you even begin the actual calculation. At least you'll know the size of the ballpark you're playing in!

✎ Even if you're not particularly visual, pictures can often help. Try translating a particularly vexing math problem into a drawing or diagram.

✎ Play around. There are often different paths to the same solution, or even equally valid solutions.

✎ When you are checking your calculations, try working *backwards*. I've found it an easier way to catch simple arithmetical errors.

✎ Try to write down all of your calculations — neatly. You'll be less likely to make a mistake if you take your time, and if you *do* make a mistake, it will be a lot easier to spot.

✎ Show every step and formula, even if you would normally skip a few. If you knew all of the principles and formulas but miscalculated near the very beginning of your analysis, you are not going to arrive at the correct answer. *But* many enlightened math teachers will take very little off if they can clearly see you knew your stuff and managed to do everything right, with the exception of hitting the right button on your calculator.

There are no "easy" tests

Some people think "open book" tests are the easiest of all. They pray for them — until they see their first one.

These are the toughest tests of all, if only because even normally "nice" teachers feel no compunction whatsoever about making such tests as tough as a Marine Corps drill instructor. *Heck, you can use your book!* Many open-book tests are also take-home tests, meaning you can use your notes (and any other books or tools you can think of).

Since you have to anticipate that there will be no easy questions, no matter how well you know the material, you need to do some preparation before this type of test:

✎ Mark important pages by turning down corners using paper clips or any other method that will help you quickly flip to important charts, tables, summaries, or illustrations.

✎ Write an index of the pages you've turned down so you know where to turn immediately for a specific chart, graph, table, whatever.

✎ Summarize all important facts, formulas, and so forth, on a separate sheet.

✎ If you are also allowed to bring your notes or it's a take-home test, write a brief index to your notes (general topics only) so you know where to find pertinent information.

First, answer the questions for which you don't need the book, including those you're fairly sure of and those you know where to find. Star the latter ones.

Next, take out your book and check up on your starred answers and erase the stars once you have answered the questions. Then work on those questions for which you must rely fully on the book.

While a take-home test is, by definition, an open-book test, it is the hardest of all. An open-book test in class simply can't last longer than the time allotted for the class. A take-home exam may give you a night or two, in some cases as long as a week, to complete.

Why are they so hard? You're *given* so much time because teachers expect that it will take you *longer* than the time available in class to finish. You may have to go well beyond your text(s) and notes to even get a handle on some of the questions, leading to some long nights at the library. Take any easy eight-hour tests lately? The longer you're given, the easier it is to procrastinate ("Heck, I've got another two nights!"), and we know where *that* leads.

There are only two good aspects to balance the scales. You've certainly been given the chance to "be all that you can be." No excuse for not doing a terrific job on a test with virtually no time limit. And, if you tend to freeze during a normal exam, you should have far less anxiety at home in comfortable surroundings.

Write on!

While I think open-book tests are the hardest ones given, I must admit I think *all* "objective" tests—including multiple-choice and true-false—are harder than essay tests. Since I suspect many of you don't agree, let me explain: I think an objective test of any kind gives the teacher much more latitude, even the option of focusing *only* on the obscurest details (which, granted, only the truly sadistic would do). As a result, it's much more difficult to eliminate areas or topics when studying for such a test (except, as noted, by using the clues the teacher has given you about the relative importance of certain topics and whatever your research into returned examinations and those from previous years has turned up).

It's also rare to be given a choice—answer any 25 out of 50—whereas you may often be given, for example, five essay questions and have to choose only three. This greatly increases the odds that even sporadic studying will have at least given you some semblance of understanding about one or two of the questions, whereas you may be lost on a 100-question true-false test.

Second, less could go wrong on an essay test—there are only three or four questions to read, not 100 potential *misreads*. I could think of a few questions, not hundreds. I'd have the time to organize (a strength) and I'd probably get points for good spelling, grammar, and writing (another strength). It's also a lot easier to budget time among three or four essays than among 150 multiple-choice.

Whether you love or hate essays, there are some important pointers to ensure you at least score better on them. Approach essay questions the same way you would papers. While you can't check your textbook or go to the library to do research, the facts, ideas, comparisons, and whatever else you need are in your own cerebral library—your mind.

Here's the step-by-step way to answer every essay question:

Step one: On a blank sheet of paper, write down all the facts, ideas, concepts, and so forth, you feel should be included in your answer.

Step two: Organize them in the order in which they should appear. You don't have to rewrite your notes into a detailed outline. Why not just number each note according to where you want to place it?

Step three: Compose your first paragraph, working on it just as long and as hard as I suggested you do on your papers. It should summarize and introduce the key points you will make in your essay. *This is where superior essay answers are made or unmade.*

Step four: Write your essay, with your penmanship as legible as possible. Most teachers I've known do *not* go out of their way to decipher chicken scratch masquerading as an essay and do *not* award high grades to it either.

Step five: Reread your essay and, if necessary, add points left out, correct spelling, grammar, and polish as much as you can. Also watch for a careless omission that could cause serious damage—leaving out a "not," making the point opposite of the one you wanted to.

If there is a particular fact you know is important and should be included but you just don't remember it, guess if you can. Otherwise, just leave it out and do your best. If the rest of your essay is well-thought-out and organized and clearly communicates all the other points that should be included, I doubt most teachers will mark you down too severely for such an omission.

Remember: Few teachers will be impressed by length. A well-organized, well-constructed, specific answer to their question will always get you a better grade than "shotgunning" — writing down everything you know in the faint hope that you will actually hit something.

Think of the introduction and the conclusion as the bread in a sandwich, with the information in between as the hamburger, lettuce, tomato, and pickle. Everything is necessary for it all to hang together, but the main attraction is going to be what's between the slices.

Worry less about the specific words and more about the information. Organize your answer to a fault and write to be understood, not to impress. Better to use shorter sentences, paragraphs, and words — and be clear and concise — than to let the teacher fall into a clausal nightmare from which he may never emerge (and neither will your A!).

If you don't have the faintest clue what the question means, ask. If you still have no idea of the answer — and I mean *zilch* — leave it blank. Writing down everything you think you know about the supposed subject in the hopes that one or two things will actually have something to do with the question is, in my mind, a waste of everyone's time. Better to allocate the time you would waste to other parts of the test and do a better job on those.

What if time runs out?

While you should have carefully allocated sufficient time to complete each essay before you started working on the first, things happen. You may find yourself with two minutes left and one essay to go. What do you do? As quickly as possible, do Steps 1 and 2 discussed previously. If you then have time to reorganize your notes into a better-organized outline, do so. Many teachers will give you at least partial credit if your outline contains all the information the answer was supposed to. It will at least show you knew a lot about the subject and were capable of outlining a reasonable response.

One of the reasons you may have left yourself with insufficient time to answer one or more questions is that you knew too darned much about the previous question(s). And you wanted to make sure the teacher _knew_ you knew, so you wrote and wrote and wrote...until you ran out of time.

Be careful—some teachers throw in a relatively general question that, if you wanted to, you could write about until next Wednesday. In that case, they aren't testing your knowledge of the whole subject as much as your ability to _edit_ yourself, to organize and summarize the _important_ points.

Read the instructions and question carefully. If you're supposed to "compare and contrast," don't just compare. If you're to analyze, don't just summarize. And if you're supposed to discuss three key reasons something occurred, don't stop at two! In fact, I would go out of my way to underline each key point in any essay that requires a specific number of ways, reasons, explanations, whatever, to make sure a tired teacher doesn't miss one and mark you down for it.

Standardized tests

The various standardized tests used in college and graduate school admissions—the PSAT, SAT, ACT, LSAT, GRE—require their own pointers. These, like my oral exams at the end of four years of college, are not specific to any course or even one grade. Rather, they are attempting to assess your ability to apply mathematical concepts, read and understand various passages, and demonstrate language skills.

Despite their ephemeral nature, you *can* study for them by practicing. A solid review of English and math is essential. If you think geometry is just for squares, you'd better change your tune! Though I've already covered multiple-choice tests, here are two specific tips for standardized tests that bear repeating: 1) Read the instructions on a previous test before you go to the test site. (There are numerous books that include "actual tests" in their prep books.) Then just skim the instructions in your booklet or on the computer to make sure nothing has changed. It will save you minutes—time that is precious indeed during any such test. 2) As far as the PSAT and SAT are concerned, there really isn't a penalty for guessing, so don't leave an answer blank!

There are a variety of companies specializing in preparing students for each of these tests—your school might even sponsor its own course, and any bookstore will probably have shelves of preparation guides.

Given their importance, I would recommend investing the time and money in any such reputable course—such as Stanley Kaplan, Princeton Review, BAR/BRI—or, at the very least, buying one of the major preparation books.

Because these are, indeed, *standard*ized tests, learning and utilizing specific techniques pertinent to them and practicing on tests given previously can significantly increase your scores, even if only because you will feel less anxious and have a better idea of what's in store for you.

If you are an avid reader and understand what you read, do well in school in most subjects, but especially English and math, and "test well," you may not feel you need such help. That's okay, too. But do note that many of the questions on these tests are word-related—"SWAN is to DUCK as YOGURT is to____"—testing both your basic vocabulary and your specific understanding of synonyms (words with similar meanings) and antonyms (words with opposite meanings).

So if you don't decide to take one of the review courses, you might still consider getting a good vocabulary book — *Better Vocabulary in 30 Minutes a Day* (Career Press, 1996) or something similar — as a study aid for such tests.

There are students who achieve exceptional test scores on their SATs and go on to compile barely adequate college records. These people are said to "test well": The testing environment doesn't throw them and they have sufficient prior experience to have an edge on the rest of the competition. Others "choke" during such tests but wind up at the top of the career pyramid.

You've probably been told for most of your life that your score on the SAT will determine whether you are a raving success eating in the finest restaurants or the busboy that cleans up afterwards. How vital is the SAT to the college admission process and, one presumes, to the rest of your life? Depending on whom you listen to, "very" or "not at all." According to Michele Hernandez, a former admissions officer at Dartmouth (quoted in the January 10, 1999 *New York Times Magazine*), "Deep down, admissions officers don't want SAT scores to count that much, but...they do." Yet in 1996, Harvard turned down 165 applicants sporting *perfect* SATs — 800 on the verbal, 800 on the math. And more than 300 colleges no longer even require the SAT or ACT for admission, believing it's more important that they assess a student's real level of learning and effort, not their "innate ability."

Though one method of predicting success, such tests are not, by any means, perfect oracles. Nor are their conclusions inalienable. Many people have succeeded in life without ever doing particularly well on standardized tests.

Important Note: As of this writing, many standardized tests are no longer offered "on paper"; they can only be taken on computer (CAT — for computer-adaptive testing — format). Among the most important that fall into this category are the GMAT (Graduate Management Admissions Test), GRE (Graduate Record Exam), and TOEFL (Test of English as a Foreign Language), along with a number of specific licensing tests.

What does this mean to you? Tests available only in CAT format require a different strategy because of two important factors: You can't return to a previous answer, and you can't skip a question and return to it later. Make sure you know if you are taking a computer or written test and practice (and strategize) accordingly! Neither the SAT or PSAT are currently offered as CAT tests. I would certainly expect them to make the transition within the next three or four years.

Epilogue

'M PROUD OF you. You made it all the way through the book. Here's my final advice:

  ✎ Reread *How to Study*, cover to cover. It's similar to seeing a movie for the second time—you always find something you missed the *first* time around.

✎ Practice what I preached. You had an excuse for flunking before—you didn't know how to study. Now you have absolutely *no* excuse.

✎ Buy, read, and put into practice whichever of the companion volumes you need.

✎ Write me a letter to tell me what helped, how much better you're doing in school, or to let me know what else I can include to add to the value of the books. Send your letters to:

      Ron Fry
      c/o Career Press
      P.O. Box 687
      Franklin Lakes, NJ 07417

I promise I'll try to respond if you ask me to, but please avoid calling me—I'll probably be on the road promoting *How to Study*! Good studying!

Index